AUSTRALIA'S Dogs

KATHERINE KOVACIC

Published by National Library of Australia Publishing
Canberra ACT 2600

ISBN: 9781922507457

The National Library of Australia acknowledges Australia's First Nations Peoples—the First Australians—as the Traditional Owners and Custodians of this land and gives respect to the Elders—past and present—and through them to all Australian Aboriginal and Torres Strait Islander people.

First Nations Peoples are advised this book contains depictions and names of deceased people, and content that may be considered culturally sensitive.

Publisher: Lauren Smith
Managing editor: Amelia Hartney
Editor: Brooke Lyons
Designer: Hugh Ford
Image coordinator: Jemma Posch
Printed in China by C&C Offset Printing Co. Ltd.

Find out more about NLA Publishing at nla.gov.au/national-library-publishing.

A catalogue record for this book is available from the National Library of Australia

CONTENTS

INTRODUCTION

Australians Love Dogs

Australians love dogs—big dogs, little dogs, fluffy couch potatoes and hardy working dogs. No matter their size or shape, we love them all. This book is both a tribute to the dogs who share our lives and a visual history of dogs in Australia, past and present. Drawn mainly from the collections of the National Library of Australia in Canberra, each photograph is a reflection of the bonds we share with our canine companions.

One of the most difficult tasks has been to decide which photographs to include. The National Library holds a vast number of pictures of Australians and their dogs, and each image tells a tale. Sometimes the story is as simple as a photographer's love for their own dog, but often it is much deeper: an epic tale of survival in harsh conditions, a comment on Australian social history or a record of a significant moment in our collective narrative. The Library's Pictures Collection is Australian life documented; a 'representative visual record of Australia's people, places, events, history, society and culture'.[1] Clearly, dogs are a key part of Australian life.

A winning team, Sydney, 1920s.

I'll pat you, hold still. Cuppacumbalong, ACT, c.1893.

What is especially significant about the majority of the Library's photographs is their historic nature. In modern Australia most of us have a camera of some sort, even if it's just in our phone. We take pictures of all sorts of things, from selfies to sunrises, whenever we see something appealing. The result can be viewed immediately on screen—and if it's not good enough, the photographer can hit delete and try again. Even if it's only an average picture, there are all manner of editing programs and effects allowing us to manipulate the original image into exactly what we want.

Photographers of the past didn't have this luxury. Each shot was carefully considered, especially by the amateur photographer. Getting film developed was quite expensive, so each frame of a 12, 24 or 36 roll of film had to be used only when it mattered. After the photographs were taken, there was a wait while the film was sent for processing. When the package of prints was finally collected, it wasn't unusual to find that a number—sometimes a large number—of the photographs hadn't turned out as desired. Blurry, over or underexposed, poorly framed ... without an easy delete function, the only solution was to throw the bad photos away, and usually the moment to take another shot was long past.

Going back a few more decades, cameras were not an everyday possession. For many people, having a photo taken meant visiting a professional photographic studio and sitting very still to allow for the long exposure time.

Yet from the moment photography was available in Australia, people wanted to have pictures of their dogs: dogs at home, at work, in formal portraits and clowning around. It is remarkable how often they appear—whether included in a group portrait with a family or a gathering of working men, posed on a chair in a photographer's studio or nestled in the arms of a woman or child. Why was it so important for Australians to have photographs of their dogs, when taking those pictures was often fraught with difficulty? It's because we've always loved our dogs. They matter to us and we want to record their places in our lives. No matter how hard it might be to get a squirming puppy to sit still, we want an image of his furry face. And when our work involves dogs, it's only natural they be included in visual records of that work.

A number of photographs in the Library's collections include a blurry dog. Sometimes the dog is only a small part of the overall image—perhaps sitting placidly to one side before suddenly deciding to have a scratch or shake or just run off the moment the shutter opens. Sometimes the dog is a key part of the photograph, and even though he's out of focus, the picture has been kept anyway—because that chance won't come again, and perhaps seeing Spot or Rex or Fifi in motion is also a reminder of the active, cheeky personality that was hiding behind that wet nose and those brown eyes.

Photographs of people with dogs also reveal information about the human subjects in the way they connect with their canine co-stars. The person who engages with the dog—through a touch, a pat, or even a smile or laugh at the dog's antics—reveals more of themselves than the person who simply shares the frame with a dog without any sign of interaction. In the same way, the dog's body language can also suggest a deeper narrative, even if it's simply the posture of a farm dog eager to get to work.

In Australia, the relationship between humans and canines was forged long before the arrival of Europeans and domestic dogs. Indigenous peoples lived here for tens of thousands of years before they were joined by Australia's first canine, the dingo. It did not take long for the dingo to find a place in many Indigenous communities as companion, protector and even part of the family. While the dingo is now viewed by many as a pest to be eradicated rather than a national treasure, it remains part of Indigenous culture and Australia's national identity.

When Europeans first arrived in Australia their dogs came too. In 1770 Joseph Banks brought his two greyhounds on Captain James Cook's *Endeavour* voyage of exploration,

An armful of puppies is guaranteed to make anyone smile.

and these hounds make a cameo appearance in the background of *Macropus giganteus, The Great Kanguroo* by Sydenham Teast Edwards.[2] The next dogs to arrive came with the First Fleet. Aboard the ships were two greyhounds belonging to Captain Arthur Phillip along with assorted puppies and at least nine other types of dogs. One of these was Hector, a Newfoundland who accompanied his owner John Marshall, Master of the HMS *Scarborough*. Not only were 'useful' dogs (dogs that could hunt) present in Australia from 1788, companion dogs came here too. Given the long and difficult voyage from England to Australia and the hardships of the early years of European settlement, a pet dog would definitely have been cherished.

Dogs appear very early in colonial art, so it's unsurprising they also feature in photographs from the moment the technology arrived in this country. The oldest photograph in the Library's collections dates to 1870 and the most recent was taken in 2022. In the 150 years that separate these two images, Australians' love for their dogs never wavered; and, as many of the photographs clearly show, our dogs have loved us right back.

The first recorded photograph in Australia was taken on 13 May 1841. The daguerreotype (an image produced on a silvered copper plate) was a view from Macquarie Place, Sydney, showing Bridge Street and part of George Street. Daguerreotypes were quite delicate, and unfortunately this image has not been located. Probably requiring an exposure time of over one minute,[3] the image was presumably of empty streets—but perhaps it included one or two dogs, asleep in the sun or in a blur of motion as they went about their canine business.

For most of the remainder of the nineteenth century, photography in Australia was a business for professionals, and an expensive hobby for enthusiastic amateurs. Then, in 1896, the Pocket Kodak was introduced to Australia. Such was the enthusiasm for photography that more than 3,000 of these cameras were sold between October and December that year. This was not the first Kodak, but it was smaller, lighter and simpler than previous cameras—and with a price of just one guinea, it allowed many average Australians to become amateur photographers. Roll-film cameras changed the nature of photography in a way that would not occur again until the advent of digital images. Now, virtually anyone could be a photographer, and they could take pictures of anything. The images these new photographers snapped were far more personal, and dogs, particularly beloved canine companions, regularly became the main subjects.

It is often thought that the unsmiling appearance of people in early photographs was due to long exposure times and a need to keep still for an extended period. However it seems that a serious expression was more to do with culture and etiquette than the mechanics of taking a photograph. Before photography became common, the only way to have a portrait made was to have one painted, and smiling portraits—particularly with teeth showing—were very rare. While today this has changed in art as it has in photography, before the twentieth century it was not considered 'proper' to be depicted with a smile. In centuries past, people in paintings who grinned widely or showed their teeth tended to be of the lower classes, or those without full control of their emotions, such as children or drunkards.[4] For everyone else, an unguarded expression might show too much, revealing emotions that were thought should remain private. Therefore, it would have been a very calculated decision to include a joyful dog—with the potential to behave in an undignified manner—in a photograph that was intended to capture a formal occasion. Not only does the inclusion of a dog reveal something about the people and their lives, but sometimes the dog even caused the human sitters to smile, or at least soften their expressions.

The twentieth century brought about a new development in photography: the informal snapshot. Cameras were now widely available and relatively simple to operate, and regardless of whether there was an amateur or a professional

Shade for the dog, Narrabeen, NSW, 1964.

Caretaker and his dog welcome a visitor to Fort Denison, Pinchgut Island, Sydney, 1930s.

behind the lens, people could be caught in unguarded moments. Often that meant smiling or laughing (and showing teeth)[5] but it also resulted in many more photographs of people playing with dogs—again showing just how much dogs were and are part of everyday life in Australia.

It is a reflection of the relationship between people and dogs—and a growing acknowledgement of the importance of canines in human lives—that dogs appear in so many photographs. It shows how integral dogs were (and are) to every aspect of Australian life, whether as part of the pastoral industry or simply as a pet in a suburban home. The picture may have been taken by a professional or an amateur, it may be posed or more candid, but a decision was made to include one or more dogs in the frame. Those behind the cameras wanted to record the role dogs played in Australian life, and there is no question that people enjoy pictures of dogs.

Australia has one of the highest rates of pet ownership in the world: 39.9 per cent of households include one or more dogs. The most recent statistics estimate there are about 5.1 million dogs in Australia, or approximately one dog for every five people, clearly showing dogs are our favourite animal companions. Less than half of Australia's dogs are purebred (40 per cent); although of the 60 per cent that are mixed breeds, an increasing number fall into the category of 'designer dog'—a specific mixture of two pure breeds. Most people (63 per cent) consider their dogs to be part of the family, and spending habits suggest a lot of dogs are very indulged. And why not? They give so much in return. Including food, healthcare and other things such as grooming, training and 'accessories', each dog-owning household in Australia spends about $2,158 on its canine members per year—an annual total of over $8 billion. It seems like a lot of money, but most dog owners would argue it's money well spent.[6]

As well as the dogs who share Australian lounge rooms and backyards, many dogs also have jobs. Farm dogs, police dogs, guide dogs and medical alert dogs are among the many working canines who make our lives better and safer.

Just like us, these dogs are happy to relax with their human mates when the working day is over. There are also canine jobs that no longer exist, such as the work of huskies in the Australian Antarctic Territory; and jobs that are less defined: military mascots and companions in adventure and exploration. All these canine roles have been photographed and the memories preserved in the Library's collections.

Within the collections there are numerous photographs of famous Australians and significant moments in Australian history that include dogs. But just as important are the photographs of the normal, the everyday and the humble. By looking through the camera lens at Australia's dogs, it is possible to see our history from a different perspective, and in that way we also see more of ourselves: what we were, and what we have become.

It could be argued that people are closer to their dogs now than ever before. But perhaps the relationship has always been this close and it is only now we are becoming more enthusiastic in expressing our love for the dogs who share our lives. There is plenty of photographic evidence in the National Library's collections to support the argument that Australians have always loved dogs. This book celebrates that love.

A soldier's best friend.

CHAPTER 1

By Our Sides

Dancer Dorothi Neil holds her poodle, Fufi, aloft at Coogee, NSW, 1962.

Dogs were domesticated at least 30,000 years ago and have been part of our lives ever since. The connection between humans and dogs has evolved throughout the millennia. Today, more people than ever live by the words 'love me, love my dog'.

Canines were the first animals to develop a permanent association with humans. For some time it was thought that domestication occurred as recently as 15,000 years ago.[1] However, there is now compelling evidence to show that dogs became domesticated thousands of years earlier, at least 32,000 years ago and possibly more than 100,000 years ago.[2] At this stage, because of the genetic closeness of the dog and wolf, it is difficult to differentiate between the species beyond a certain evolutionary point. Although the original domesticate would have been a wolf ancestor, it is hard to pinpoint when the domesticated wolf became the domesticated dog.

Apart from determining precisely when dogs were domesticated, the most intriguing question for many is: why did dogs and humans form a bond in the first place? Forming an alliance with a species skilled in tracking and hunting would have benefited ancient humans, but the benefits would originally have been countered by the aggressiveness of 'protodogs' (primitive wolves that gave rise to the domestic dog as we know it today) and the need to feed them. After all, if food is scarce, there is no advantage in attempting to domesticate an animal that will need to be fed.

In fact, it seems unlikely that dog domestication was the result of a conscious human decision.[3] Instead, it is entirely possible that dogs were domesticated due to a sense of kinship between two species—so in effect, 'humans domesticated dogs, and dogs domesticated humans'.[4] Some evidence of that kinship can be found deep in the Chauvet Cave in France. Preserved in the floor of the cave are the footprints of a child, together with the paw prints of a large dog.[5] The tracks indicate they were walking together, and other markings made by the child have been dated to 26,000 years ago.[6]

Essentially wolves may have domesticated themselves, and some of the physical changes that have appeared in dogs over time—such as floppy ears and curly tails—tend to support this theory of self-domestication: the friendliest animals have an advantage and, somehow, that friendliness drives changes in physical characteristics.[7]

Naturally, once domestication had occurred humans found dogs could be more than just companions: they could also make life better by acting as guardians, aids in hunting, and even load carriers. The relationship between dogs and humans continued to evolve throughout the millennia.

Definitive proof of cat domestication is only 4,000 years old.[8] So for ancient humans, there was never a question of being a 'dog person' or a 'cat person'; dogs and humans were a team for thousands of years before cats were even a consideration.

Throughout the centuries, people and dogs have remained close. The human–dog relationship is recorded in written and oral histories, and in art from ancient civilisations through to the modern age. The concept of a pet—an animal that has no specific task beyond that of close companion—is not new. However, pet keeping was once the preserve of the elite upper classes. It was only in the sixteenth and seventeenth centuries

Carlo gets a hug, sitting between sisters Ruby and Pearl Easdown, 1908.

Mr Webb's dogs, Victorian goldfields, 1850s.

that it became acceptable for people in the next tier of society (what would later come to be known as the middle class) to own pets. This was particularly the case in British towns and cities, where it was the breeding and quality of the animal itself that mattered, rather than any supposed job it might have. By 1700 it was clear that people were dedicated to their pets, although displays of overt affection towards dogs (and cats) did not become respectable for ordinary people until the nineteenth century.[9]

The rapid expansion of the middle classes in the nineteenth century also meant an increase in the number of pet dogs, partly because more people could afford them. This also coincided with a dramatic increase in the number of different dog breeds. The fashion for any particular breed of dog was driven by the British upper classes. Whatever they had, the middle classes wanted too, and anything that was in vogue in Britain was highly desirable in colonial Australia.

As the socially aspirant middle classes quickly discovered, the presence of a purebred dog gave the owner prestige: '[N]obody who is anybody can afford to be followed about by a mongrel dog'.[10] A purebred dog reflected well on the person who held the other end of the leash. Colonial Australia's beginnings as a penal colony meant that well-to-do Australians were also sensitive to notions of good breeding. In an 1869 edition of *The Australasian*, one writer concluded his letter regarding Gordon and Irish setters by saying:

> *Melbourne and the neighbourhood is overrun with a lot of half-bred brutes that are a discredit to the colony, and it is a pity that the whole brood cannot be swept away and their places filled by dogs that have some pretensions to the names they bear.*[11]

In the same way that a breed today can gain popularity through its association with a celebrity or even a movie, in the nineteenth century, owning the same breed of dog as the queen or another member of the aristocracy afforded a degree of social cachet. Queen Victoria's widely known love for animals contributed significantly to the popularity of dog ownership, and a desire for particular breeds. Her dog, Dash, made the already popular King Charles spaniel an even more attractive companion. Pekingese—an exotic and rare 'new' breed in 1860s England—were closely associated with Queen Victoria (her dog's name was Looty), the Duchess of Richmond and, later, Princess Alexandra. The Russian wolfhound (borzoi) was another breed brought to prominence in Britain by Queen Victoria and Princess Alexandra.

As it did with many British tastes and fashions of the nineteenth century, Australia soon followed the trend of pet dog ownership, and breeds that were popular overseas also found favour here. Colonial paintings show that in addition to the more utilitarian types of dogs (such as deerhounds, sheepdogs and terriers) some companion breeds had already found their way to Australia.

In the second half of the nineteenth century, Australians began to show what real dog people they were. The bushman and his dog were already becoming the stuff of legend, but now the city dog was also part of many Australian families. Dog shows were not only an opportunity to proudly parade one's beloved canine, they were also a way to showcase new breeds. Britain's first dog show took place in 1859, and the first recorded Australian dog show was held in Hobart, Tasmania in 1862.[12] Victoria quickly followed with a dog show in 1864, and from that point they became regular events throughout Australia. The fact that the first Victorian show had almost 400 entries indicates both the level of dog ownership in the relatively young colony and the pride people felt for their canine companions.[13] In a strange way, dog shows also embodied the Australian spirit of equality and a fair go: in these competitions, an average person with a good dog could quite easily beat a wealthy socialite.

Dogs of many different breeds were imported into Australia in the nineteenth and early twentieth centuries, and Australians found that some weren't suited to the

Some winning cocker spaniel entries, with their judge, at the Sydney Royal Easter Show, c.1900s.

Philanthropist Philip Wollen shares a special moment with Lamoo, Pippa and Joe.

environment. In the outback, pastoralists and stockmen developed dogs specifically to work in Australian conditions: the Australian cattle dog, the Australian stumpy tail cattle dog and the kelpie (see chapter 3). For most people, these are the breeds that spring to mind as quintessentially Australian dogs, but there are several others that are proud Aussies (see chapter 4).

At different times, various breeds have held the title of Australia's favourite dog, including Labrador retrievers, German shepherds and Staffordshire bull terriers. However it seems that, in true Australian fashion, the dog most likely to be found in the average home is a mixed breed of some description. There has been a recent surge in the popularity of 'designer dogs'—a specific mix of breeds such as a labradoodle (Labrador retriever cross poodle) or a puggle (pug cross beagle)—but often the best description of a dog's lineage is cross-breed, bitzer, Heinz or even mutt. The point is, it's not really important. For most of Australia's dogs and their humans, what is important is the connection they share: the human–dog bond.

The Human-Dog Bond

The human–dog bond has been the subject of considerable scientific interest in recent years, although groundwork for this research was done by scientists in the mid to late twentieth century. Dogs, above all other animal species, have forged a special bond with humans. Any dog owner today—or from centuries past—knows the relationship they share with their four-footed mate is something special. There is now plenty of scientific evidence that not only supports this, but confirms the psychological, social and even physiological benefits of living with a companion animal.

Essentially, the human–dog bond is founded on similar behavioural and physiological processes to attachments formed between two people. This means that in some cases, the bond between a person and their dog may be just as strong and important as any other significant relationship in their life.

Research also shows that spending time with companion animals—particularly dogs and cats—is linked with good health. Lower blood pressure and cholesterol are two examples of the physical benefits associated with pet ownership. In fact, when it comes to reducing stress, the presence of a pet dog or cat is more effective than the company of a spouse or human friend.[14] One study showed that following a heart attack, people with pets—particularly dogs—have a much higher chance of being alive after one year. Scientists have also established that pets have a positive impact when people are coping with chronic health conditions and illnesses including cancer, heart disease and dementia.[15] And it's not all one-way: just patting a dog causes a significant lowering of blood pressure in both the human and the canine.[16]

Living with a dog also has a positive psychological impact. Playing and interacting with a dog creates joy and pleasure in a stressful world. As a human family grows up and evolves through events such as children moving out, divorce and even death, a dog will be a constant, reliable companion. Dogs also lead to more social contact and new friendships, and they foster a sense of community: strangers are more inclined to talk to a person who is walking a dog, and the dog park or beach is the perfect place for people to connect, talk and share information as they watch their dogs playing (even if it seems people at the dog park are more likely to recognise the names and traits of other dogs than to learn the names of other people).[17]

It's not always entirely clear why dogs are good for our health. Living with a dog tends to encourage a person to exercise more, but not everyone who has dogs takes them for regular walks. Yet some health benefits are evident regardless of the human–canine exercise level.

Salty sea dogs Lee Murray and his Airedale terrier, Peter, at Rushcutters Bay, NSW, 1931.

A moment of shared joy in Gundagai, NSW, c.1900.

Dogs have complex thoughts and feelings. Not only are they good at reading human behaviour and body language, they communicate with us in many different ways. Communication and understanding are key to our relationships with dogs. Most Australians who have a dog didn't set out to improve their health; they wanted a companion who—at least to some degree—understood them.

Across Australia every weekend, many people and their dogs walk in parks or enjoy a coffee and puppacino at a local cafe, and thousands more participate in a dog sport or activity of some kind. A large number are involved in conformation showing, presenting their dogs to be judged against others of the same breed and a written breed standard. Media coverage of dog shows usually focuses on the primping and preening of dogs, but these events are far more than just beauty contests: judges consider many factors, including movement, anatomical structure, health and temperament.

For those who want to help their dog learn good manners and perhaps a trick or two, there are plenty of good instructors to help them. Most people take their dogs to obedience classes as a way of having fun together, with the added bonus of learning something while also strengthening the human–dog connection. It's also possible to compete in obedience trials and a variety of other canine sports. Some of the most common competitive dog sports include agility, rally obedience, freestyle to music (often called doggy dancing or dances with dogs), canine disc (where dogs and their handlers compete in events such as choreographed frisbee catching), and tracking, herding and retrieving trials. Often the human competitors involved in these canine sports didn't originally set out to compete; they acquired a dog, then found a fun way for their dog to use their abilities. For these people, and for the tens of thousands of Australians with dogs who don't compete in canine sports, the most important thing is simply sharing life with their four-legged mates.

Artist Joy Hester hugging Tommy and Brother.

Double exposure: Meg, Felicity and Moya Coyle with their dog (and his ghostly twin) in the sitting room at Woodbridge, Double Bay, NSW, c.1925.

The Bond Captured

Searching through the National Library of Australia's Pictures Collection, it quickly becomes clear that Australians have cherished their dogs and celebrated the human–canine relationship for well over a century. Dogs have been captured in candid moments and posed for the camera—sometimes with all the accessories of the grandest nineteenth-century studio portrait. Even when the dog in question didn't remain still while the photo was taken, many pictures have been kept, showing just how much the dogs mattered.

One family photograph in the Library's collections (at left) seems to include two dogs: one quietly gazing out from beneath a couch, the second not much more than a blurry dog shape lying on the rug. This apparently accidental double exposure could have been discarded and a new picture taken. Instead, the photo was retained and continues to delight almost a century later.

The importance of dogs is also evidenced by photographs taken of dogs in places where we might not expect to find them. There are many pictures of dogs in the remote outback, but also at bush hospitals, playing with a prison inmate in the 1930s and cradled in the arms of a German man at the Holsworthy Internment Camp, New South Wales, during World War I (page 39). Dogs are ubiquitous in Australian life.

Some of the most attractive—and revealing—photographs are the candid pictures that include both human and dog. In these images, it is often possible to catch a glimpse of the bond between the two: the companionship and happiness that comes from living with a dog. The joy on a child's face, the touch of a hand on a dog's back (or a paw on a human leg), a glance from person to dog or the subtle body language that is clear evidence of a close relationship; these are the pictures that speak to the heart of the human–dog connection.

Perhaps one of the things that makes canine companionship so appealing is that dogs never judge. A dog doesn't care if you live in a mansion or a hut; the type of car you drive and the clothes you wear are irrelevant; and if you make a mistake, a dog is very forgiving. The story behind the photograph of 'Digger' George Henry and his dogs exemplifies the human–canine bond.

According to newspapers of the time, George Henry served with the 9th Battalion during World War I.[18] He first appeared in newspapers around 1924, when he was walking from Melbourne to Cairns—although he had actually started in Adelaide in 1923, intending to walk around Australia. Described as 'attired for the road, with a swag up',[19] Henry was not the sort of person who would usually attract attention; in fact, as a swaggie, he was the sort many would turn their backs on. What made Digger Henry stand out was his dogs.

Sometimes wrongly described as dingoes, Henry's pack of mixed breeds was trained to perform various tricks—as well as carry a swag and billy—and their performances earned enough money to keep man and dogs going. Henry apparently got the idea from the trained dogs he saw in France and Belgium during the war. By the time he reached Townsville in 1924, he claimed to have tramped across a good portion of Australia, his faithful dogs at his side. The story evolved while Henry and his pack were on a walk from Adelaide to Cairns and back: now the dogs were all dingoes, found as pups in a hollow log in Queensland and caught and tamed by Digger Henry. He then taught them the tricks that delighted people as they passed through each town. The idea of performing dingoes (rather than dogs) may have come from Henry himself, or the newspapers—but no doubt it fuelled interest in the man and his furry troupe. In the photograph on page 43, it is clear there is some dingo ancestry behind at least one of these dogs—and kelpie influence is also evident—but they certainly didn't come from the wild. Possibly Henry had a pure dingo or two with him at some stage during his travels, as the number of dogs travelling with him varied over the years. When he returned to Adelaide in 1926, Henry had three dogs with him—Tom, Sailor and Con—and he had travelled more than 19,000 kilometres.

Even in the worst of times, a dog brings happiness to a German detainee at Holsworthy Internment Camp, c.1918.

A boy and his dog wharfside at Darling Harbour in Sydney, c.1925.

Tom was apparently the star of the show. Digger Henry crafted a clever trick for him to perform that involved the dog following a scent, and resulted in a shilling for Henry every time. Digger Henry would cover Tom with a chaff bag (to make sure he couldn't 'cheat' by seeing or smelling anything) then ask someone in the crowd to donate a shilling, which would be returned if Tom failed. Digger then passed the coin to one of the children in the crowd, with instructions to hide it inside a nearby shop. When this was done, Tom was told to 'find the shilling' and with no hesitation he did just that.[20] For a dog trained in scent work it would not have been difficult—Digger Henry had handled the coin, which meant Tom had a familiar odour to seek—but it must have looked very impressive, and presumably netted plenty of donations on top of the original shilling.

It is possible that, as a returned serviceman, George Henry was suffering from what today is known as post-traumatic stress disorder and found it easier to be out on the road than constrained by four walls. He clearly had a close relationship with his four-footed mates, and because other people were also drawn to his dogs, he was able to earn enough money to live in the way he chose. Digger Henry enjoyed training his dogs and was good at it. The presence of his dogs, wearing signs and carrying things, made him approachable and resulted in social contact he otherwise might not have had. The sign worn by the dog on the right of the photograph reads (in part):

> *My name is Digger Henry I neither bite nor steal.*
> *I am travelling 'round Australia ... master and family*
> *... kelpie and dingo ... that is well known ... kindly help*
> *me on ... to Adelaide town.*

Digger Henry's tale is a colourful one, but all the photographs in this book have stories behind them—and at the centre of each story is the bond between Australians and their dogs. City or country, purebred or bitzer, companion or highly trained police dog—it makes no difference. The settings and poses also vary dramatically, and the photographs could be examined for details of Australian history, fashion and taste. But once again, these details, while fascinating, are not the real story. Every dog has been captured on film because of his or her relationship with a person: usually either the one behind the lens or the one sharing the frame. Beyond the type of dog and the what and where of the photograph's origins lies the literal heart of the story. So even if a picture simply shows a canine silhouette in an empty landscape, there is no photograph that could be considered to show *just a dog.*

A stop along the way for Digger Henry and his travelling companions.

CHAPTER 2

The Dingo

Australia's only native canid, the dingo.

Many people think of dingoes as quintessentially Australian dogs, yet technically they're not the same as domestic dogs. Today these ancient migrants, Australia's largest wild mammalian predators, are known throughout the world.

The evolutionary path and taxonomic classification of the dingo has been a controversial issue for decades. In 1793, the dingo was identified as a distinct species, *Canis dingo*, and many scientists maintain this is still the most accurate classification.[1] Others argue that the dingo is an ancient type of domestic dog and should be known as *Canis familiaris* (Dingo).[2] While debate continues over the most appropriate taxonomic name, new research shows that genetically, the dingo genome is structurally and evolutionarily different from domestic dog breeds.[3] The dingo is unique: a truly wild canid and an Australian icon.

The first written report to mention dingoes was made in April 1623 by Dutch navigator Jan Carstensz. Carstensz was on an expedition commissioned by the Dutch East India Company, and after travelling south along the coast of New Guinea, his ships, *Pera* and *Arnhem*, entered the Gulf of Carpentaria. Several times when going ashore, Carstensz recorded seeing dingo tracks and, significantly, he reported the canine pawprints as occurring together with human footprints, suggesting the dingoes were associated with Aboriginal people. On one occasion, Carstensz also mentioned seeing 'great numbers of dogs'.[4] It was another 65 years before the next recorded sighting, made by William Dampier.

However, the history of the dingo in Australia reaches back much further than these white explorers' observations.

The Dingo's Mysterious Arrival

How dingoes got here remains unclear. Possibly they arrived in Australia on foot, crossing a land bridge from islands to the north; either wild animals moving independently, or partly domesticated, walking together with humans.[5] However it's more likely dingoes arrived thousands of years ago by boat, accompanying seafaring hunter-gatherer people from South-east Asia.[6] Whether such people were part of waves of human migration or simply transient traders remains unclear. And if they brought the dingo, was it as a commodity to be bartered? Or was there another reason, such as a shipwreck, that dingoes found themselves on Australian shores? If dingoes arrived in this way, they must have been tame enough to travel safely in small boats with people, but also possess the physical and behavioural traits that enabled them to thrive in the wild in Australia.

Fossil evidence—ranging from individual elements such as teeth and bones to full skeletons—goes some way to helping track the dingo in Australia. Fossilised remains have been uncovered in a variety of locations including Victoria, New South Wales and Western Australia, and together they show that dingoes were not only present in Australia by around 3,500 years ago, they were widespread throughout the country. Many researchers believe this is conservative, suggesting an arrival date over 5,000 years ago: just because older evidence hasn't yet been found doesn't mean dingoes weren't here.[7] Effectively, the known fossils don't represent the earliest dingoes in Australia, but rather indicate the species had formed a stable population large enough to become visible in the archaeological record.

The proposed timing of the dingo's arrival also corresponds to the regional extinction of two of Australia's major marsupial predators. The Tasmanian devil (*Sarcophilus harrisii*) and the Tasmanian tiger (thylacine; *Thylacinus cynocephalus*) became extinct on the Australian mainland between 3,500 and 5,000 years ago but continued to exist in Tasmania, a place the dingo never reached. Although evidence suggests the dingo was not solely responsible for these extinctions, competition from another predator would have had a significant impact.

That the thylacine and the Tasmanian devil continued to exist in Tasmania provides another clue to the timing of the dingo's arrival in Australia. Around 12,000 years ago, rising sea levels caused Tasmania to be cut off from mainland Australia. As the dingo has never inhabited the island state, we can assume they did not arrive on the mainland until after this separation had taken place, isolating and preserving the devil and thylacine populations.

John Gould's 1863 drawing is more fox-like in appearance, but identifies the animal as a distinct species, *Canis dingo*.

Genetic research has attempted to shed light on the origin of the dingo. Genetic data supports an arrival date between 3,000 and 5,000 years ago and suggests an Asian origin for the dingo's ancestors (East Asia or South-East Asia). Dingoes and domestic dogs differ genetically in several important areas,[8] and some of these differences are so significant they can be used to determine whether an individual dingo is a pure or hybrid animal. This has important implications for dingo conservation in Australia, as there is now a genetic test that can indicate whether an individual animal is a domestic dog, a hybrid or a pure dingo. This means hybrid animals can be identified and removed from the wild, and that zoos and wildlife sanctuaries can maintain and build up pure dingo bloodlines. Ultimately, it may be possible to restore dingo populations to some areas of the Australian wilderness, although it will be necessary to balance the benefits to the species and the ecology with the potential impact on livestock farming.[9]

As well as suggesting an arrival date, the archaeological record indicates that since its arrival in Australia, the dingo has remained true to type. A near-complete dingo skeleton found at a site in the Murray–Darling Basin was reconstructed and dated to around 3,000 years ago. By comparing this skeleton with those of present-day dogs and dingoes, and the fossils of early Asian *Canis* species, it was concluded that dingoes are different to domestic dogs; dingoes across the continent are skeletally the same; and the structure of the dingo has remained unchanged for thousands of years.

Isolated in mainland Australia, there was no selective breeding by humans (such as has occurred with domestic dog breeds) and no interbreeding between dingoes and any other type of dog or wolf. The dingo was the only canid here, and it adapted perfectly.

Even thugs have soft sides: standover man Walter Tomlinson shows off his dingo-cross in Sydney, 1931.

Dingoes in sanctuaries, such as these at Billabong Sanctuary in Nome, Qld., play a vital role in conservation education and preservation of the species.

BROOKE

Erecting the dingo-proof fence in western Queensland, c.1963.

The War on Dingoes

Since white settlement, the dingo has been much maligned. From the very first moments of colonisation they were considered a problem—a pest that stood in the way of pastoral expansion. Many early colonisers set out to make the native canid extinct. In an 1856 account of John Batman's settlement of Port Phillip, an incident was recorded in which Batman came across a dingo that was tame and therefore obviously a companion of the local Aboriginal people. However when the dingo refused the colonisers' attempts to pat it, the response of Batman's group was to shoot the animal.[10] White colonisers also found that killing companion dingoes was an efficient way of disrupting Indigenous communities. In 1840, squatter Samuel Rawson recorded in his diary that after he had killed dingoes belonging to Indigenous people, their owners:

> *buried the dead bodies of their four legged companions with great ceremony, wrapping them in blankets and sheets of bark and lighting fires by their graves after which they decamped and proceeded about 1/2 a mile further up the river.*[11]

Sadly, this has been the dingo's fate ever since. From the Dingo Fence to bounties for each dingo shot, and widespread baiting with poisons such as 1080 (sodium fluoroacetate), the dingo has remained constantly under threat. Unlike most native Australian animals, the dingo is one that people have tried to demonise and destroy rather than celebrate and preserve.

While dingoes do present significant problems for some livestock farmers, wild dingoes do not actively seek confrontation with humans and many people believe they should be protected: not just for their unique evolutionary place, but also for the valuable role they can play in maintaining natural ecosystems and eradicating introduced pests such as foxes and feral cats.

As with other wildlife, problems occur when habitat is lost, foreign species are introduced, and humans encroach on what was once dingo territory, upsetting the natural balance of the ecosystem. For example, dingoes were once prevalent in the scrublands of Victoria's Mallee region, and scientists have argued that ongoing attempts to eradicate the dingo, combined with the introduction of other predators, has led to a decline in the population numbers of many small to medium-sized native animals.[12] Native grasses also seem to benefit from the presence of dingoes, and where dingoes exist, animal species with an adult body weight of between 5 and 100 kilograms (such as red foxes and kangaroos) are less abundant. The implication is that by suppressing predators (such as foxes and feral cats) and large herbivores (kangaroos), dingoes have a positive impact on populations of smaller mammals, resulting in a more balanced ecosystem.[13] In addition, by controlling kangaroo numbers in a particular area, more feed is available for livestock, benefiting farmers.[14]

Dingoes can now be found in most mainland habitat types, and across all mainland states and territories. While dingoes are usually associated with the hot, arid deserts of central Australia, they are also found in rainforests, wetlands, grasslands and even alpine regions. Dingoes are not found in densely settled areas and are far less common on the southern side of the Dingo Fence, a barrier approximately 5,600 kilometres long that stretches from near Jimbour in the Darling Downs region of Queensland to the Nullarbor Plain, just above the Great Australian Bight in South Australia.

Describing the Dingo

The fact that dogs and dingoes can interbreed—and from the time of early white colonisation, attempts were made to do just that—is one of the reasons it can be so difficult to identify what distinguishes a pure dingo from a dog–dingo hybrid.

Dingoes are about the same size as a medium-sized domestic dog, always lightly built and with minimal fat.

Evolved for speed and agility, the dingo has a long, straight back and powerfully muscled hindquarters. The dingo's head is large in proportion to its body and the skull longer than it is wide. Strong jaws and a highly flexible neck provide efficiency when hunting both small (rodents and insects) and larger prey. Comparisons made between the skulls of modern dingoes and similarly sized domestic dogs have revealed a number of significant differences.[15]

We tend to picture dingoes with exclusively ginger or sandy-coloured coats, but pure dingoes can also be cream/white or black and tan. Most dingoes are also likely to have some white points—toes, feet, tail tip or chest patch—although this is not always the case, and the amount of white in the coat varies greatly between individuals. The ginger colour is by far the most common, with shades ranging from a deep rust to pale buttery cream. Deeper ginger or red shades provide some camouflage against the reddish sands of central Australia while lighter ginger shades blend with dry grasses.

The texture of a dingo's coat depends on the habitat and the season, ranging from a thick double coat in winter in the mountainous south-eastern regions of Australia to a wiry single coat in the tropical regions of the far north.

Behaviourally, the dingo exhibits several traits that align it more closely with primitive canid species, such as the wolf, than the domestic dog. Dingoes form long-term pair bonds—that is, a male and female remain together from one year to the next. In a dingo pack, only the dominant male and female breed, and there is only a single breeding season (and, therefore, one litter of pups) per year. All members of a pack help look after the pups, a form of care generally uncommon in domestic dogs.

Despite a popular misconception, dingoes are capable of barking: they just don't bark often. They have a range of vocalisations, barking only in limited situations, and, like other canids, also communicate using body posturing, facial expressions and scent.

Bunjil and his dingo helpers in Djabwurrung cave paintings, Black Range, Victoria.

Dingoes hunt both cooperatively and as solitary animals. As opportunistic predators, dingoes eat more of what is common and easy to catch in any given environment. Rabbits, wallabies and small mammals are a regular part of their diet, but wild dingoes normally eat a range of other things, including insects, birds, reptiles and plants. They will also feed on carrion and livestock, especially sheep and goats. However one study indicated dingoes prefer to eat kangaroos even when sheep and cattle are abundant.[16] Unlike domestic dogs, dingoes cannot easily digest meat with a high fat content, which may be a factor in the perceived dingo preference for kangaroos over sheep as a food source.

Dingoes and Indigenous Peoples

The dingo is an important part of the life and Dreaming of Indigenous peoples in many areas of Australia. According to Bradley Smith, the dingo is unique in Dreaming stories in that the first time the dingo appears, it is already in the form of a dog-like creature, whereas many other animals and ancestral beings go through some sort of transformation.[17] Together with the rainbow snake, the dingo is one of the most represented creatures in First Nations Dreaming.[18]

Dingoes in rock art are rare compared to many other Australian animals, although a number of images do exist. There are several near-life-size charcoal depictions located at a site in the Wollemi National Park, New South Wales, and paw print stencils are present in both the Northern Territory and New South Wales. Dingoes are depicted in association with humans in a few locations, such as in the Laura region of Queensland and in Kakadu National Park, Northern Territory.

Where dingoes are represented, their polychrome colours, large size and central placement indicate these animals were of considerable importance. At Mutawintji National Park in western New South Wales, there are

As with other unique Australian animals, early depictions of the dingo often lacked accuracy.

NATIVE DOG OF NEW SOUTH WALES.

a number of stencilled dingo paw prints in the same shelters as many human hand stencils. According to Mutawintji traditional owners, these dingoes would have been the favoured companions of people camping in the area. In the Black Range, Victoria, a small rock shelter in a granite boulder contains rock art that is not only unique in Victoria (and possibly all of Australia), but also one of the most significant cultural sites in south-eastern Australia. It is a depiction of Bunjil and his two dingo helpers (page 58). Bunjil is an anthropomorphic, supernatural being who produced many features of the landscape and led each tribal group to their territory. He is associated with the making of medicine men, the initiation of novices into manhood and the revealing of secret knowledge.[19] Because it is difficult to accurately date rock art, these and other depictions of dingoes are unfortunately of little help to researchers attempting to pinpoint the timing of the dingo's arrival in Australia.

Although Indigenous peoples were without canine companions for thousands of years, once dingoes arrived it seems many communities swiftly incorporated them into almost every part of life, culture and spirituality. The relationship between the dingo and these communities is a unique example of the human–animal bond. While the dingo's pre-arrival history remains vague, the knowledge and traditions of Australia's First Nations peoples are central to understanding what came after. Exploring the relationship between dingoes and people enriches our knowledge of both Indigenous culture and dingoes themselves.

The dingo experience—the way they established a connection with First Nations peoples and became integrated into communities, families and skin-name systems—may help provide a broader understanding of how today's domestic dogs' ancestors came to share their lives with humans over 30,000 years ago. However it is important to appreciate that because of the richness and sheer diversity of First Nations cultures, the human–dingo relationship varies between different communities across the country.

If dingoes were already at least partly tame when they first arrived in Australia, their incorporation into Indigenous peoples' lives would have taken place quite rapidly. This in turn would have resulted in the dingo's faster dispersal throughout the continent, as the animals travelled with people and were perhaps traded with different communities. Historically, dingoes were obtained from the wild as pups and brought back to camp where they lived among the community. This meant there was never any selective breeding or ongoing efforts to domesticate; each generation of dingoes came from the wild.

The name 'dingo' was used by people living in the Port Jackson area of New South Wales at the time of European settlement and derives from a local Aboriginal term for tame camp canines.[20] However, across Australia, different language groups have different names for the dingo, and also use different words to distinguish tame camp animals from their wild counterparts.[21]

For many Indigenous peoples, dingoes are traditionally regarded as individual members of the community. They are given names, food and shelter, but also have to obey social rules. For example, in some communities, dingoes may be expected to follow women and be prevented from accompanying men to ceremonies.[22] For other people, such as the Yarralin community in the Northern Territory, some of the rituals and knowledge surrounding dingoes are entirely the men's domain.[23]

The dingo's incredible ability to find water is an important contribution to community life, although this aspect of kinship with the dingo is sometimes considered secret knowledge:

> *Individuals will carry with them 'dog dreaming', that is, they are the custodians of the law and history of dingoes and dogs. Much of the law as it pertains to dogs remains secret and is often held in the hands of only a few in the community.*[24]

Artist George French Angas captures the connection between a Nauo woman and her dingo companion, in Port Lincoln, SA, in 1845.

There are many dog Dreaming sites located throughout Australia, each with a story of the creation and movement of the dingo through country.

Dingoes, like domestic dogs, are often considered to be part of the family. They are treated with great affection and afforded respect when they die, and anyone harming another man's dingo is courting trouble. Often an individual dingo will become one person's favourite, receiving more care and attention than other dingoes living with the community.

Indigenous people had been successfully hunting for tens of thousands of years before the dingo's arrival, and did not change their strategies too much simply to incorporate their canine companions. However, dingoes proved to be very useful in the quest for food. An image of a dingo painted in a rock shelter at Keep River in the Northern Territory is a tribute to one of these particularly good cooperative hunters.[25] In some communities, dingoes help in the quest for food by accompanying women and children as they forage, perhaps contributing meat from opportunistic kills or participating in hunts for small and medium-sized animals.[26] Their keen sense of smell helps locate hiding animals (for example, in a burrow or undergrowth), and they can also flush or trap them. On a hunt that requires stealth, the presence of dingoes could prematurely frighten the target so, when working together, dingoes weren't used as persistence hunters. However, dingoes were commonly used in many cultural regions to assist in large, organised game drives: helping the 'beaters' (usually women and children) drive game towards the armed hunters, preventing game from escaping in the closing stages of a hunt, and helping to seize the animals.[27] The dingo's role in food sourcing highlights its important place in daily life for many First Nations communities.

Dingoes serve as defenders against evil forces, or the physical threat of human or animal intruders. For the Walmadjari people of south Kimberley, an important function of the dingo is to warn of approaching evil spirits.[28]
For the Yankunytjatjara people living near the Everard Ranges

in the far north of South Australia, dingoes act as watchdogs, collectively defending the entire camp and with individuals protecting the area around each human shelter. It has also been suggested that for many communities, such as the Yankunytjatjara people, strong affection for puppies is one of the reasons for keeping dingoes.[29]

Dingoes are also a way of keeping warm: huddling up with dingoes can provide protection against cold desert nights. Even using a dingo as a lapdog means a bit of extra warmth, particularly for older members of a community.[30] Of course, a dingo must have been raised from puppyhood to tolerate this and be useful as a canine blanket.

Dingoes living in Indigenous communities are also very helpful for cleaning up scraps and all manner of waste around a camp site, although some people believe having dingoes around would simply create more mess. Perhaps the idea of dingo as camp cleaner remains unresolved because this was not a reason that was important in determining whether a group chose to allow dingoes into their community. None of the roles tame dingoes occupied in Indigenous peoples' lives seem to be essential so perhaps, like the modern domestic dog, the bond between dingo and human has always been one of emotion rather than necessity.

Dingoes are important in the life and Dreaming of First Nations peoples, but their exact role varies across the continent.[31] The dingo is associated with the supernatural more than any other animal represented in Dreaming narratives. This can be seen in rock art which sometimes depicts the dingo as a go-between, linking the human and spiritual worlds, accounting for its ability to warn of evil spirits. In the Dhurga language of the Yuin people of New South Wales' South Coast and Southern Tablelands, the word 'warrigal' means 'wild dog'. The warrigal appears in creation stories and plays a significant totemic and spiritual role in culture.[32] According to Deborah Bird Rose, the Yarralin people in Victoria River, Northern Territory, believe that humans have dingo origins.[33] In other communities, dingoes were buried in a similar way to people; at one burial site, human remains were placed in the centre of a large number of hearths (fireplaces) with five canids (presumed to be dingoes) buried at the perimeter of the site, suggesting that the animals continued to protect their human companions in the spirit world. Archaeological evidence of dingo burials in sites across southern Australia as well as in Arnhem Land provide further evidence that dingoes and First Nations people have long shared a special relationship.[34]

The dingo is embedded in First Nations culture; life would not be the same without it.

Conservation

Dingoes and farmers have been in conflict since the arrival of European colonisers with their desire for pastoral expansion. Yet despite the war on dingoes, the impact of wild dog predation of livestock has not lessened over the years.[35] Part of the problem can be attributed to feral domestic dogs and dog–dingo hybrids; but to prevent the pure dingo from ultimate extinction, it is clear that new ways to resolve the conflict must be found. There are several solutions that may help to reduce the need for lethal control of wild dingo populations, including barrier fencing, a form of visual deterrent called fladry, the use of flock guardian dogs such as Maremma sheepdogs, and some tolerance in regions where populations of largely pure dingoes are found.

Dingoes affect the environment in ways that go beyond their potential impact on the livestock industry. In Australia and elsewhere in the world, it has been shown that the removal of apex predators (such as dingoes, wolves and lions) can impact an entire ecosystem. As a result, the idea of restoring predator populations as a means of conservation has gained considerable support.[36] The most consistently documented effect dingoes have is limiting the populations of the larger native animals, particularly kangaroos, that are their preferred prey. Soon after European settlement, farmers were noting that when they decimated the local dingo population (via a campaign of poisoning or shooting) the result was a rapid increase in the number of kangaroos. In response to this, the settlers then began to target the kangaroos, leading to an ongoing persecution of both carnivore and herbivore to the environment's detriment. A number of recent scientific studies confirm that when measures are taken to control or eliminate dingo populations, there is an increase in the abundance of kangaroos.[37] Large kangaroo numbers can present a significant problem for farmers, competing with livestock for food and damaging crops. But if the presence of dingoes helps manage populations of native herbivores, vegetation is likely to be more abundant and in better condition, reducing conflict with the farming industry. There is anecdotal evidence indicating dingoes help control populations of feral goats, deer and pigs, again proving to be a benefit to the ecosystem.

There is also some research that suggests attempts to cull dingo populations may actually increase attacks on livestock.[38] Dingoes limit their own population densities (for example, by having only a single breeding pair in a pack). When individual dingoes are killed, disruption to the social hierarchy may result in an increase in dingo numbers and a breakdown of territorial boundaries, leading to an increase in livestock predation.[39] It seems that finding ways to coexist with dingoes may provide benefits to livestock enterprises.

Traditional owners, including the Bundjalung, Yuin Walbunja and southern Yuin tribes, have expressed concern that there has been no engagement with Indigenous communities when developing current dingo management programs (such as baiting or other means of culling). As the dingo is part of First Nations heritage—'a significant Aboriginal cultural feature of the landscape'—they have called for a moratorium on dingo control and a formalised consultation process to protect the dingo's cultural importance.[40]

Fighting for the survival of an Australian icon at a World Environment Day rally, Melbourne, 2004

Yawning, not snarling: a dingo shows off its powerful jaws.

One of the biggest threats to dingoes is dilution of the pure gene pool through hybridisation (with domestic or feral dogs), but they are also put at risk through factors such as exposure to disease; the increasing isolation of pure populations resulting in inbreeding; and programs designed to eradicate wild canids, regardless of whether they are dingoes or feral dogs.

The dingo's future depends on the work of various conservation sanctuaries throughout Australia. The people at these sanctuaries are dedicated to saving the dingo and preserving pure bloodlines for the future. Keeping dingoes in captivity is not ideal and poses a number of challenges, but at the moment such practices are essential if the gene pool is to be maintained and other conservation plans put into action.

Despite problems when dingoes and pastoralists clash, it is a fact that after at least 4,000 years in isolation on this continent, the pure dingo is a native animal—one of Australia's most recognisable animals—with an important place in the environment. As Roland Breckwoldt stated, 'not everything in Australia was designed only for human benefit'.[41]

CHAPTER 3

On the Farm

A rare moment off and time for a scratch under the chin in Alice Springs, NT, 1961.

When Australia's wool industry was at its peak and the economy was booming, it was often said that the country rode on the sheep's back. But perhaps it was actually the dogs on the sheep's backs and at the heels of cattle that enabled Australia to become a primary producer of international importance. Without dogs, there is no way Australian farmers of the nineteenth and early twentieth centuries could have managed flocks and herds in such vast spaces. Despite today's mechanical and technological advances, dogs continue to be an integral part of life on a working farm.

In the early colonial days, settlers kept any cattle, pigs or sheep in small fenced enclosures close to their homes. Animals were let out to graze during the day and brought in at night, so the only dogs necessary were guard dogs to protect livestock from dingo attack—or, more likely, theft—and even they were in short supply. In a letter to Joseph Banks written on 9 May 1803, New South Wales governor Philip Gidley King stated:

> *We are very much in want of a breed of shepherd's dogs to watch our increasing flocks of sheep. If such a thing could be procured, it would be of great use to this colony.*[1]

With the crossing of the Blue Mountains in 1813 and the opening of the western road in 1815, colonists had access to vast, unfenced areas on which to graze stock—and they quickly found the dogs they had were not up to the job. It was hard to round stock up, let alone drive the animals long distances to the saleyards in Sydney, and the problem became worse as pastoralists pushed further into Australia's interior.

Sheep numbers rose sharply. In 1861 there were over 5 million sheep in New South Wales, but ten years later there were 16 million. Further south, during the decade after the colony at Port Phillip was established, the surge in sheep numbers was even more dramatic. Wool growing was a major contributor to the economy prior to the discovery of gold. Not only were sheep numbers increasing, so too were the sizes of agricultural holdings. By the second half of the nineteenth century, in parts of New South Wales there were properties covering over 800,000 hectares. Wire fences were erected, but the areas enclosed were still vast. There was a need for a dog that could handle Australia's heat, as well as work sheep and cattle that were virtually running free.

Australia's first sheep and cattle dogs were types imported directly from Great Britain. However, the hotter climate and vastly different vegetation meant that breeds such as the Scotch collie (now generally known as the rough or smooth collie) and the old English sheepdog were not well suited to working in Australian conditions. Other types of dog, in particular the working dogs that ultimately gave rise to the border collie, adapted very well indeed.

Most dog breeds known today were developed quite recently. While it appears that ancestors of the various different types of working dogs existed in particular regions of the United Kingdom, they were not viewed as specific breeds. Dog books of the early nineteenth century such as *Cynographia Britannica* (1800) and *The Sportsman's Cabinet* (1803) simply refer to 'shepherd's dogs'. It was from these dogs that the border collie was developed. Illustrations from the period show a type of dog that bears a considerable resemblance to the modern border collie, and even 200 plus years ago, these dogs were known for their intelligence. Both *Cynographia Britannica* and *The Sportsman's Cabinet* include the same anecdote about a man accused of sheep stealing

Pushing up the flock: dogs were essential in the establishment of Australia's pastoral industry.

A ute-load of enthusiastic workers ready for the National Sheep Dog trials in Canberra, 1964.

to illustrate the shepherd's dog's cleverness. During the man's trial, the court was told of his modus operandi. The accused would pose as a buyer and ask to view a mob of sheep. He would take his dog with him and, as he moved through the flock, the man would give subtle signals, letting the dog know which sheep were wanted: about a dozen animals from a flock of several hundred. The 'buyer' would then leave and that night, from several kilometres away, he'd send the dog back alone. The dog would pick out the individual sheep that had been pointed out earlier, separate them from the flock and drive them 'a distance of ten or twelve miles, till he came up with his master, to whom he delivered his charge'.[2] Although it may be greatly exaggerated, the story brilliantly highlights the skill of sheep and cattle dogs.

Border Collie

While not an Australian breed, the border collie must be mentioned here for the role the breed plays on farms throughout Australia. The border collie's ancestors originated several hundred years ago in the border region between Scotland and England, bred by local shepherds specifically to handle livestock in difficult terrain.

The first recorded border collie to arrive in Australia was the bitch Hindhope Jed, who arrived in 1901. Although Jed's coat was shorter than that of the rough border collie known today, newspaper images show a black-and-white dog with a head and body closely resembling the modern breed. Jed was owned by Messrs King and McLeod who are best remembered for their role in developing the kelpie. At the time, Hindhope Jed's breed or type was generally recorded as a 'collie' 'smooth-haired collie' or 'sheepdog' when she was entered in working dog trials, or when advertisements were placed to sell her progeny.[3] Occasionally she and one or two other black-and-white working dogs were referred to as border collies,[4] and King and McLeod were using this name in their advertising by 1904, although it would not become official for some years.[5] Hindhope Jed was eight years old when she won the 1903 Sydney sheepdog trials, but even prior to her arrival in Australia, she was apparently 'a noted performer in Scotland and New Zealand'.[6] *The Australasian* reported that:

> *She will do any class of work, is an excellent yard dog, and has no superior in forcing sheep into trucks or into a shed; will bark as much as much as desired, and when called upon to do so will heel cattle equally as well as a cattle dog. She will also "hunt away" in any direction.*[7]

Clearly, there was no shame for local dogs being beaten by such an experienced and capable working dog.

Australian owners and breeders began to show border collies (as opposed to entering them in working dog trials) early in the twentieth century, but a national standard for the breed was not adopted until 1963. Highly intelligent, the border collie is still the dog of choice for many Australian farmers, but as with the other working breeds, border collies can also excel at activities such as agility and obedience where their energy, loyalty and desire to work can be used in other ways.

Several unique dog breeds have arisen in Australia, and perhaps the best known of them all are the kelpie and the Australian cattle dog (sometimes referred to as the blue/red heeler or Queensland heeler). These two breeds are irrevocably linked with life on the Australian farm and in the outback. The stories of their origins—how they came to be developed specifically for Australian conditions—are a fascinating part of Australian history.

Kintyre Moy and his handler, W.J. Clifton, win the 1949 Cooper Sheepdog Trial by a resounding 28-point margin.

Binnie begins the morning commute to work, Taminick, Vic.

Kelpie

There have been many theories and half-remembered tales put forward about the kelpie's origins. Researchers such as Tony Parsons have expended considerable energy and time sorting fact from fiction.[8] For example, in his 1914 book, *Australian Barkers and Biters,* Robert Kaleski wrote that the kelpie 'comes from the cross of a Fox and a Black Smooth Collie made by a gipsy for a poaching dog a hundred years ago'.[9] A respected Australian authority on dogs, Kaleski's views featured regularly in newspapers and magazines of the day. Not only had he already confidently expressed this theory several years earlier, but he continued to uphold the idea for decades. Many argued strongly (and correctly) against the idea that foxes formed part of the kelpie's ancestry, but because of the public's high regard for Kaleski, the notion gained widespread support.[10]

As well as the fox theory, it was also suggested the breed already existed in Scotland before it was imported to Australia in the early 1800s. While a particular strain or type of dog may have been used by Scottish breeders, the kelpie was most definitely developed in Australia. Similarly, although some early breeders experimented by crossing dingoes with collies, the dingo does not appear to have contributed to the development of the kelpie breed.[11]

Even aside from these myths, the story surrounding the who, when and where of the kelpie's beginnings was, for many years, a muddle of conflicting dates and a bit of hearsay mixed in with the facts. The difficulty in pinning down the kelpie's origin partly arose because the breed was not developed consciously; that is, no-one set out to create a new breed of working dog. Instead, it was a matter of mating dogs—mostly smooth collies—who showed the greatest ability for working stock.

One fact that has never been in doubt is that the working dog Australia knows today began with a man named John 'Jack' Gleeson and his prized bitch called Kelpie.

The Gleeson family arrived in Sydney in 1844 when Jack was just two years old. They subsequently moved to Victoria where the extended clan became well-established. In 1867 when Jack was 25, he was working up on the Glenelg River in south-west Victoria, on William Murray's Dunrobin station, a vast property of more than 63,130 hectares.[12] Jack Gleeson had a keen eye for horses and dogs, and at some point he became aware of the exceptional sheepdogs being worked on nearby Warrock station. He made it his mission to acquire one of those dogs.

The canines in question were two pure collie sheepdogs, imported in 1867 from Scotland by George Robertson, owner of Warrock station. When the collies were mated, Gleeson was desperate for one of the hardworking Robertson-bred dogs, and he tried a number of times to buy a female pup with no success; they simply weren't for sale. Robertson did, however, give a female pup to one of his relatives and in 1869 that young man was ultimately prevailed upon to exchange her with Gleeson for a very good horse. Gleeson finally had his Warrock dog and he named her Kelpie, apparently after a shapeshifting spirit of Scottish folklore.[13]

Kelpie was described as:

> *an ordinary looking well-bred collie of fair size, long-haired and with lop-ears that went up when at work. She was brownish black on back and sides with some white on breast, and a little about the face and under her lower jaw, and had tan legs.*[14]

Gleeson left the district not long after acquiring Kelpie, working his way north. In the western Wimmera, he spent time on Ballarook station, training Kelpie to work sheep during the shearing season.

After his time on Ballarook, Gleeson headed for the Lachlan River district of New South Wales and a property called North Bolero, where he was to take up the position of overseer. But on the way, he stopped off to see a mate,

Mark Tully, who was managing a station near Urana. Tully was also a dog man, and he gave Gleeson a young male dog called Moss. Moss was a prick-eared dog with short black fur, bred on Yarrawonga station on the Murray River.

The Yarrawonga dogs came from excellent Scottish lines. In 1865 John Rutherford, who had arrived in Port Phillip with his family in 1848, arranged for his brother back in Scotland to send some of the Rutherford's special sheepdogs to him at Yarrawonga station. The dog and bitch—Clyde and Lassie—became famous throughout regional Victoria for their skill working sheep. Moss was one of their pups.

With his pair of well-bred working dogs, Kelpie and Moss, Jack Gleeson continued on to North Bolero station, located not far outside the town of Ardlethan. It was here the first Kelpie–Moss litter was born around 1872–1873. Gleeson mated Kelpie and Moss at least twice, always giving pups to friends and apparently never selling any. Unsurprisingly, the pups proved to be good working dogs and were highly regarded. However, it was when Gleeson's Kelpie was mated to a dog called Caesar that the foundations of the kelpie breed were truly established.

By this time Gleeson and his dogs were residents on yet another Riverina station, and Caesar lived on an adjoining property. Like Kelpie, Caesar was a dog of distinction. His sire and dam were Brutus and Jenny, collies imported from Scotland in 1870 by Gilbert Elliot and William Allen of Geraldra station, Stockinbingal. Brutus and Jenny mated during the long trip, and Caesar and his littermates were born shortly after the ship arrived in Australia. In 1871, Brutus won the working dog trials at the inaugural Burrangong Pastoral and Agricultural Show, held in Young. A report in the *Australian Town and Country Journal* described Brutus' performance as:

> *[S]omething wonderful. Three sheep were let loose and taken outside the ground, and the dog, upon the word being given, brought them into the ground, and across through the crowd of people, running*

Kelpies keep things running smoothly in the saleyards at Homebush, NSW, in 1925.

here, there, and everywhere in a manner which would confuse a human being, to their pen, without even as much as a bark. So uncommonly well did this shepherd's friend behave himself that the other competitors resigned all claim to the prize, and would not put their dogs upon trial.[15]

With such distinguished parentage, it is not surprising Gleeson thought a Kelpie–Caesar match would produce talented sheepdogs. The litter was whelped in 1875 and, as with previous litters, Gleeson gave the pups away to friends. One of the lucky recipients of a Kelpie–Caesar pup was Charles T.W. King, nephew of John King of Wollongough station, near Ungarie, New South Wales. King's pup was a prick-eared black-and-tan bitch that he named Young Kelpie; she would later become known as King's Kelpie.

Four years later, King's Kelpie cemented her reputation and that of the entire Kelpie lineage when she tied for first place in the 1879 Forbes Pastoral and Agricultural Show's inaugural sheepdog trials. Interest in the trial was high, with men travelling over 240km to witness the event. Despite continuous rain, hundreds of people stood transfixed as the competition played out over six hours.[16] Seven dogs contested the prize, each required to drive three sheep into a pen with their masters using only voice and gesture to guide them. It came down to King's Kelpie and a dog called Tweed. The judges decided to test the dogs with a single sheep. Kelpie put in splendid work bringing the sheep up to the entrance of the pen, but it refused to go in. According to *The Burrangong Argus*, it was here that Kelpie really showed her skill:

Whichever way the sheep turned, the dog's nose was there, but Kelpie neither got mad herself nor made the sheep mad by her mouthing: it was simply an exhibition of the higher intelligence one animal possessed over the other. At last Mr King retired

A smiling kelpie-type dog seems to know he's an important part of this group, Gundagai, NSW, c.1900s.

Two Elfinvale Stud kelpies hitch a ride with founder Tim Austin in 1967.

from his post just outside the hurdles into the far corner of the pen—the sheep backed one step towards him till just within the hurdles, and then Kelpie almost shoved her in a corner. The trial was complete—and tremendous cheering rang out from the onlookers who waved their hats and umbrellas in approval of the wonderful sagacity the dog had show all through.[17]

The same article reported that although the judges called the competition a tie based on the skill of the dogs, Tweed, unlike Kelpie, did not manage to pen the sheep.

King turned down offers to buy Kelpie and instead began to breed her. Initially, dogs bred from King's Kelpie were known as 'Kelpie's pups' but, by the turn of the century, they had simply become 'kelpies'. After Charles T.W. King triumphed with Kelpie at the Forbes trial, it was his cousin, Charles Beechworth King, who truly pushed ahead with the development of the breed. The latter formed a partnership with Alexander McLeod, setting up a kennel on Wilgar Downs station near Nyngan, New South Wales, with the intention of breeding kelpies. A 1902 advertisement for their kennel begins, 'Kelpies - Bred Pure from Imported Stock 1871 - The Original Line of Kelpies... All other strains of Kelpies are bred from these'.[18] Even as late as the 1950s, other breeders were still advertising dogs for sale with reference to the King and McLeod lines.[19]

As the kelpie strain of dogs became more widely known and sought-after, a number of different pastoralists imported dogs from the Rutherford kennels in Kildonan, Sutherland, Scotland. This was the same kennel that bred the ancestors of Moss, the sire of King's Kelpie. It is believed the Rutherford line of collies was created from a mixture of the best dogs available from shepherds in the north-western highlands of Scotland and the border region of Scotland and England. This combination of strains produced dogs that had the qualities required for Australian conditions.

Rutherford collies continued to be imported in the early twentieth century, and no doubt some of them contributed to the kelpie gene pool. Gerald Kempe, the man who introduced the kelpie to South Australia, acquired his first kelpie, Saxon, in 1886. In the following years he purchased more kelpies from interstate as well as importing Rutherford dogs. A 1910 article in Adelaide's *The Register* reported that Kempe had just secured a third pair of Rutherford collies for South Australia.[20] The kelpies he bred were instrumental in establishing the breed's popularity in South Australia.

Kempe was tireless in his promotion of quality working dogs. In a contribution to *The Australasian* newspaper's 'Kennel Gossip' column, Kempe observed that the kelpie was such a success because the breeders of the kelpie strain of working dogs had not considered colour, coat type or any other detail except the best working ability. In this way, they had developed a type of dog that had the best instincts and build for good sheep work, as well as 'keen eyesight, activity, and low, silent, wide and watchful working'.[21]

Today, natural ability is still regarded as the most important attribute for breeders of working kelpies to consider. Of course, a working kelpie should look like a kelpie, but superficial qualities that may matter in the world of dog shows are irrelevant. The working kelpie is a medium-sized, strongly muscled and agile dog possessing a smooth gait, good length of stride and the ability to turn at speed and use the crouching, stealthy movement necessary for working sheep. These basic requirements are the result of generations of selection for dogs suited to the physical demands of working sheep for long periods. Kelpies should have great stamina and a strong instinct and talent for working sheep both in yards and in open country. A friendly, open nature is essential, as is a good balance between the high activity needed for work and an ability to relax: kelpies who are overly excitable or nervous do not make good working dogs. Overall, the kelpie is a highly intelligent dog with an alert, eager and loyal nature.

The coat is generally flat and moderately short. Most people think of the kelpie as a red dog, with the colour ranging from chocolate to light red, possibly with tan markings. However kelpies can also be black with or without tan, any shade of fawn or tan, and even a grey-blue colour. If tan markings are present, there may be a little or a lot, and they can be any shade of tan, from dark to light.

Ultimately, it's not the colour of the dog that matters; it's what he or she can do with a flock of recalcitrant sheep.

Australian Cattle Dog

Queensland heeler, blue heeler, red heeler ... regardless of the name, every Australian recognises the distinctive Australian cattle dog. Like the kelpie, this breed was developed in Australia for Australian farming conditions, and both breeds are national icons. But while the kelpie was developed from Scottish sheepdogs, the Australian cattle dog—or Hall's heeler, as it was originally known—was a completely new breed.

The Hall's heeler came into being decades before the kelpie. Around 1825 a group of young men, mostly colony born, began to establish cattle runs in the Upper Hunter Valley. Among them was seventeen-year-old Thomas Simpson Hall who, together with some of his brothers, established two properties in New South Wales: Gundebri, near what would become the town of Merriwa, and Dartbrook, near Aberdeen. Thomas Hall took over the management of Dartbrook and remained there for the rest of his life. He also oversaw the management of the Hall family's accumulated free and leasehold properties, controlling over 404,000 hectares.

Hall and his men faced long and difficult journeys when driving cattle to and from market and between remote properties. Thomas Hall recognised the dangers associated with working with half-wild, horned cattle as well as the problems associated with moving them through terrain that could be harsh and sometimes treacherous, so he set about establishing two breeding programs on Dartbrook. The first was to develop polled (hornless) cattle, and the second was to breed a cattle dog that could stand up to the difficulties of the Australian climate and landscape. By 1840, Hall had achieved both objectives, and the dog he'd developed was so perfect for the job that for the remainder of his life he did not alter it in any way.

When he began his quest for a dog suited to Australian conditions, Thomas Hall first looked to the dingo. It had the hardiness, endurance and heat tolerance that was so lacking in the working dogs imported from England and Scotland; all he needed was the right sort of dog to cross with the dingoes he already had at Dartbrook. He decided to import a strain of dogs found in Northumberland, in the border region between England and Scotland; an entirely different type to the sheepdogs already present in the colony. Although its origins are obscure, historians have named the type the Northumberland blue merle drover's dog. It was not uncommon for different farming regions of Britain and Scotland to have their own distinguishable strains of working dogs, and as the Hall family hailed from Northumberland, it's not surprising this was where Hall turned when he sought a good working dog. Records confirm that droving dogs with a mottled blue coat had been selectively bred for colour and working ability on the Hall family farm near the Scottish border.[22]

No records survive regarding Thomas Hall's breeding program, but after acquiring Northumberland blue merle drover's dogs, he began to selectively cross them with dingoes to achieve the balance of traits he was seeking. The result was the Hall's heeler.

Once he had the type of dog he wanted, Hall's breeding program would have been very large as he worked to provide his dogs to all the stockmen on the various Hall properties. The ongoing success of the Hall family in the cattle industry was closely intertwined with skilled dogs that made moving large herds over vast distances so much easier.

Farm dog Bo takes a flying leap up to the back of a truck at Moorabool, Vic., 1991.

It's likely that Hall's heelers were not generally available outside the Hall pastoral empire while Thomas Hall was alive. However, when Hall died in 1870, the family trust was wound up, land and stock were sold and the dogs began to gain wider attention. The name Hall's heeler would also ultimately disappear; such was the skill of these dogs that they simply became known as 'cattle dogs'.

No doubt a number of stockmen from the former Hall properties continued to breed dogs from the Hall line after 1870, but today only a few names are known. At the time, rural Australia was also evolving. More fencing, smaller farming selections and the expansion of the railway system in New South Wales meant the nature of long-distance droving was changing. Cattle dogs were still working in the country, but as the nineteenth century drew to a close, they also began to find favour with city dwellers. It wasn't long before cattle dogs made their way to the show ring.

Selecting dogs for the show bench rather than working ability usually works to a breed's detriment. In the case of the Australian cattle dog, the main advantage gained was the requirement to maintain more complete records of pedigrees and bloodlines. Naturally enough, given its origins on Hall properties throughout New South Wales and Queensland, in the early twentieth century the Australian cattle dog first began to appear in agricultural shows in and around Sydney and Brisbane. The breed was not exhibited in Victoria until the 1930s, with other states to follow.

There were some differences between the cattle dog populations in Queensland and New South Wales. In particular, red cattle dogs were far less common in Queensland while the incidence of naturally tailless dogs ('stumpy tailed') was much higher than in the southern population. This may have been because particular characteristics were preferred (and actively bred for) in the different states, or simply a side effect of selective breeding on various Hall properties. For example, if a line of exceptionally skilled and intelligent working dogs happened to be largely stumpy tailed, that characteristic would be expected to show up in more progeny.[23]

Breeders in both states bought dogs from each other. Many Sydney dogs headed north during the 1930s, resulting in a decrease in cattle dogs of purely Queensland ancestry. However, while New South Wales bloodlines may have been achieving overall dominance, the preference of some Queensland breeders for the tailless attribute meant that dogs descended from the early Queensland lines survived in stumpy tail cattle dog breeders' kennels.

In 1903, a breed standard drawn up by Robert Kaleski was published in *The Agricultural Gazette of New South Wales*. He described the general appearance of the cattle dog as 'that of a small, thick-set dingo',[24] but the main characteristics were those recognisable in the breed today: a head that is broad between the ears (which should be short and pricked); dogs about 50 centimetres tall with females a bit smaller; and a short, smooth, very dense coat. The acceptable colours were:

> *Head black or red, with white stripe down forehead preferred; tan spot over each eye; body, dark blue for choice on back, sometimes with black saddle, black spot on tailbutt; lighter blue on under parts; legs red, tan, or blue; other eligible colour, red speckled.*[25]

Tails were to have a slight brush, not be too long in relation to body length and not be carried too high; Kaleski's breed description made no allowance for a tailless cattle dog. Yet by 1917 there were enough stumpy tail dogs for separate classes to be held in a number of Queensland dog shows.

Interstate differences continued to simmer, with various standards being put forward in both Queensland and New South Wales over the following years. At one point, stumpy tailed dogs were included in a Queensland standard but specifically excluded in New South Wales. Perhaps partly due to this disagreement over tails, Kaleski's early breed

An Australian cattle dog holds a Jersey herd in place without causing stress.

First lesson for an Australian cattle dog pup: the introduction.

standard was not universally applied. As a result, breeding was somewhat inconsistent, and many proponents of the working cattle dog believed the quality of dogs declined during the interwar period.

Following the end of World War II, not only was a consensus reached regarding the breed standard of the Australian cattle dog, but just as importantly, one outstanding dog had a lasting impact on the breed. Little Logic was born in August 1939 in New South Wales and was sent to noted Queensland breeder Arch Bevis. Little Logic's own pedigree was incomplete; but there were numerous highly successful New South Wales cattle dogs in his line, and Little Logic seemed to inherit the best from each of them. Bevis heavily promoted the dog (and his own Hillview Kennels), and Little Logic ultimately sired 140 pups. According to Noreen Clark, '[D]escent from Little Logic to the Australian cattle dogs of today is via twenty-four of his offspring'.[26] By the end of the 1950s most pedigreed Australian cattle dogs probably had Little Logic somewhere in the family tree.

Today, the Australian National Kennel Council's standard for the Australian cattle dog no longer suggests the dogs should resemble thick-set dingoes. Instead, the general appearance should be 'that of a strong compact, symmetrically built working dog, with the ability and willingness to carry out his allotted task however arduous'.[27]

Although stumpy tail cattle dogs were far more common in Queensland, their numbers began to decline greatly due to the preference for New South Wales dogs and other issues impacting on the type. By the 1980s the breed had become very rare and was on the path to extinction. However, in 1988, the Australian National Kennel Council decided to implement a rescue program. While there was only a single registered breeder at that time, the Council believed that a reasonable number of unregistered purebred stumpy tails existed and that with careful selection, they could be used in a breeding program to revive the stumpy tail cattle dog.

Along with the stumpy's tail (which should naturally be no longer than ten centimetres) there are several other subtle differences between the Australian stumpy tail cattle dog and the Australian cattle dog—but dogs of both breeds are alert, courageous, loyal and extremely intelligent, with a natural talent for controlling and moving cattle.

Together with the kelpie, the Australian cattle dog and Australian stumpy tail cattle dog are national icons, recognisable as quintessentially Australian even to those people who profess to know little or nothing about dogs. But beyond this, these are the dogs that made Australia, facilitating the development of a pastoral industry that made this country the envy of the world.

Smithfield

Although not originally developed in Australia, the Smithfield is a type of working dog that—since its arrival in the 1800s—has become an essential part of Tasmania's canine heritage. Smithfields take their name from London's Smithfield Livestock Markets, where such dogs were used for droving animals to and from market. The Smithfield Markets closed in June 1855, and new cattle markets were opened on the northern edge of the city in Copenhagen Fields, within the Borough of Islington. This meant nineteenth-century London was being supplied with meat from processing yards and abattoirs located outside the city centre, and there was no longer a need for drovers' dogs at Smithfield. Yet it seems they were needed elsewhere and, perhaps surprisingly, they found their greatest supporters on the other side of the world, in Tasmania.

Walter Beilby mentions the breed as 'Smithfield Cattle Dogs' in *The Dog in Australasia*, Australia's first dog book. However, he confuses them with the old English sheepdog, believing the name 'Smithfield' was just something applied in parts of Queensland, Tasmania and New Zealand.[28]

Moofty the Smithfield helps bring lambs up to market in Dairy Plains, Tas.

William Smith with his Australian koolie, Nell, in Canberra, c.1906.

Despite the misunderstanding, his reference to Smithfield confirms the dogs were being bred in Australia in the nineteenth century, and while not suiting the working conditions in some parts of the country, they did not simply die out. In fact, there was plenty of interest in the breed.

A letter published in *The Australasian* on 14 October 1882 from a reader in Baringhup, Victoria, inquired whether the Smithfield was better for working cattle than the Scotch collie and asked for information about Smithfield breeders.[29] An answer came in November:

> *Sir, In your issue of the 14th inst., a correspondent is asking information respecting stumpy-tailed cattle dogs, or Smithfield. I am, and have been, a breeder for some years, having imported direct from England ... They make first-class cattle dogs, and are, I think, more suitable for the work than the Scotch collie. – W.A. Forster, Stonehenge, Eastern Marshes, Tasmania.*[30]

The modern Smithfield is a medium-sized dog with a medium-length, somewhat shaggy coat. They are not heavy dogs, but rather possess a strong, agile body and average around 47 to 53 centimetres high at the shoulder. The coat can be almost any colour (or colour combination); grey and white, black and white, tan or cream seem to be most common. A gene mutation means Smithfields may have a natural bob tail (as indicated in Mr Forster's reference to stumpy tailed cattle dogs) but when a tail is present, it is covered in shaggy fur. Folded ears frame a face characterised by a bright, inquiring expression. With a stable, confident nature and a willingness to work, the Smithfield is an active, intelligent dog, devoted to his human family.

The Smithfield still has a presence in Tasmania (and on some properties in mainland Australia). Although the breed is not recognised by the Australian National Kennel Council (or any of the state canine bodies) there exists a band of dedicated people determined to preserve the true Smithfield type. This task is made more difficult by those hoping to make money passing off bearded collie crosses (and probably other cross breeds) as true Smithfields.

Each year, Smithfield fanciers throughout Australia and sometimes from other countries travel to the Campbell Town Show in rural Tasmania to celebrate this hardy working dog. There's always a good entry in the various classes and dogs are presented in their natural condition; this can mean anything from washed and brushed for the occasion to 'just off the farm' with muddy legs and the odd grass seed stuck in the fur. The most important criteria is that all dogs entered must be genuine working dogs.

With no official recognition or registry, it seems the Smithfield survives because they are great workers—true farm dogs with even temperaments—and farmers know a good dog when they see one.

Australian Koolie

A working breed developed in Australia, the koolie is not widely known, but for those familiar with these hardy dogs there are none better.

At some stage during the 1840s or early 1850s, a distinctive type of sheepdog arrived in Australia with settlers from Germany, finding their way particularly to agricultural areas in South Australia and south-western Victoria. Originating in Southern Germany (including alpine regions) these dogs all had distinctive merle-patterned coats, which earned them the nickname 'tiger'.[31] The dogs were not well suited to the hotter, dryer Australian conditions, but the German settlers interbred their dogs with other working dogs and gradually developed their own line, which they traded and shared among family and the wider settler community. DNA testing confirms koolies are a distinct breed, but also that they share part of their heritage with another Australian dog, the kelpie.

The name seems to have evolved from 'collie' and it is not uncommon to see the breed referred to as a German coolie. However, as these dogs do not exist in Germany, the name Australian koolie is more accepted, honouring the breed's true country of origin.

The koolie is briefly mentioned as part of a discussion of Australian dogs in a 1901 edition of English magazine *The Field*:

> *[T]he German collie — a wall-eyed merle ... He gets his name from a very good working strain owned by a German and imported from the Fatherland many years ago. The strain is prized for their good works and I know it is popular in the back country.*[32]

Koolies are strong, athletic dogs ranging in height from 45 to 65 centimetres at the wither with bitches a bit smaller. The variation in height is broad simply because the koolie is so adaptable, and different bloodlines have been bred larger or smaller to best suit particular work. Prick ears are most common although koolies with drop ears also occur. The coat can be smooth, short or medium in length, and colour varies from solid red or black, bicolour, tricolour, red merle or blue merle; the most important thing is that the dog can be easily seen by both the handler and the herd.[33]

Although the appearance of individual koolies can vary greatly, what matters is a dog's ability to carry out the work he was designed for. This means a good koolie should have great stamina, a build that enables him to work with speed and agility, and a strong herding instinct. Loyal, intelligent and highly trainable, the koolie is a great all-rounder and an asset on any farm.

The Koolie Club of Australia was formed in 2000 as a means of both registering the dogs and enabling breeders to track dogs and make the best decisions for the future of their bloodlines. There is no specific breed standard and no intention to have the koolie formally recognised as a breed able to be shown in the conformation ring. The primary aim is simply to continue to breed and improve what has long been an excellent working dog.

Kangaroo Dog

Although not technically a breed, the kangaroo dog or Australian staghound was an important part of Australia's colonial history. Originally a cross between a purebred Scottish deerhound and a greyhound, the kangaroo dog's purpose was hunting—whether for kangaroos, wallabies, emus or (later) rabbits. While they were sometimes also used as watchdogs, they were bred for speed, agility and the ability to catch 'game'.

This type of dog still exists today and they are generally known as staghounds, however there is no such thing as a purebred, and no widely recorded genetic lines. In fact, many different types of breeds are crossed to produce modern staghounds; the only requirement seems to be medium to large size, suitability for hunting and a good temperament.

Kangaroo dogs were used for hunting a variety of animals, including emus.

AUSTRALIAN SPORTS.--HUNTING THE EMU.

CHAPTER 4

Other Australians

Australian terrier Mickie needs a little help sitting still for the camera.

The quiet Australians—the lesser-known dog breeds developed in this country—are loved by many. All of them were bred to work, but today are just as likely to be part of suburban households, hanging out with their human families or turning their considerable intelligence and athleticism to other pursuits.

Australian Terrier

The Australian terrier, originally known as the rough or broken-haired terrier, was possibly the first breed developed in Australia. Assorted terriers were likely among the first dogs to arrive in Australia, with one author noting in 1827 that 'a little short-legged terrier' was useful when hunting kangaroo: apparently a hunter could quickly lose sight of deerhound and greyhound-type dogs at full gallop, but it was easy to follow a short-legged terrier trailing after the pack.[1]

Details of the Australian terrier's early history have been lost, but the type arose in the early 1800s (probably in Tasmania). Using a variety of different terriers, early breeders were after a keen hunter of vermin, a watchdog that barked an alert when necessary, and a good companion. British breeds that may have contributed include the Dandie Dinmont terrier, Manchester terrier, Skye terrier and the old Scotch terrier (an ancestor of the modern Scottish terrier).

In 1889 the Australian Rough-coated Terrier Club was established and a breed standard drawn up. At the time, it was noted that the fledgling breed was 'the progeny of the Scotch terrier altered by judicious interbreeding with relative strains and the effects of a hot climate'. The aim of devising a standard was to establish a correct type given that 'some of the prize winners at past shows were somewhat incongruous in appearance'.[2] Walter Beilby, author of Australia's first dog book, was slightly more blunt in his assessment, stating 'I have not the slightest hesitation in pronouncing these dogs arrant nondescripts'.[3] But the rough-coated terrier type was already one of the most popular breeds in the country—both as a hardy working dog and as a pet—and with the persistence of the Club, breeders were brought into line and began to consistently breed terriers that were true to type. At the beginning of the new century, the breed's popularity was continuing to climb. In 1901 noted dog show judge F. Freeman Lloyd penned a series of articles for *The Field* in which he commented on the dogs he saw while visiting Australia. Of the local terrier he wrote:

> *These dogs are, however, very plentiful, possess 'type', and are game and excellent ratters. If one cares to take a stroll on the esplanade at St Kilda, the suburban and seaside resort of Melbourne on a Sunday, he may observe as many as forty to fifty following the enjoyment-seekers. From this one can easily see they are in great requisition as companions, and I have noticed many carried as lap dogs by ladies in carriages.*[4]

A revised standard drawn up in 1896 was very similar to that of the present-day Australian terrier, the main difference being that the earlier standard specified a greater weight range (3.6 to 6.5 kilograms, compared to 6.5 kilograms for dogs and slightly less for bitches today). The 1896 standard also allowed dropped as well as pointed ears. In 1947, a more detailed standard was adopted. Today, the Australian terrier should have a harsh, dense, double coat with a ruff around the neck and a topknot on the head. They can be completely sandy or red in colour, but are most well known with a two-colour coat: steel blue, blue or dark grey-blue body with rich tan on the face, ears, lower legs, feet and under the body. Ears are pricked and the tail is set and carried high. Most importantly, the Australian terrier is long in proportion to height (around 25 centimetres at the withers for dogs and slightly less for bitches); it is best described as a 'sturdy low-set dog'.[5] Australian terriers are loyal, intelligent little dogs, full of spirit and courage but with an even nature that means they are easy to train, good with children and wonderful companions.

Australian Silky Terrier

The Australian silky terrier appeared in the late nineteenth century during the more haphazard breeding years that would ultimately give rise to the Australian terrier. As well as the rough-coated terrier type that was emerging, there was a second type with far softer, silky fur. At some stage, the Yorkshire terrier was introduced to the breeding program for dogs of this type to improve the texture and length of the soft coat. In the 1890s the two types were still considered variants of the same breed; at dog shows, both were categorised and judged as Australian terriers, but split into rough-coated or silky-haired groups. The silky-haired type was refined in Sydney, and initially the little dogs were known as Sydney silkies.

The Victorian Silky and Yorkshire Terrier Club was formed in 1904, and it was this club that drew up the first breed standard. Newspaper reports indicate a Sydney club may have formed at about the same time; officially, though, the Sydney Silky Terrier Club was established in 1906 and devised its own standard.[6] It was not until the 1950s that the state clubs reached an accord and the breed was officially recognised as the Australian silky terrier.

A silky terrier dog can be about the same size as her Australian terrier cousin—23 to 26 centimetres at the shoulder—and is compact and refined, but with enough substance to suggest she could hunt and kill rodents as originally intended. The silky has a fine bone structure and usually weighs somewhere between 3.6 and 5.4 kilograms, although the official standard simply states weight should be in proportion to height. Unsurprisingly, the blue and tan coat is silky—flat, fine and glossy—with a natural part down the centre of the dog's back. Although the fur is long, it must not be long enough to impede the dog's gait; it should be possible to see daylight underneath. Pricked ears and a tail carried high gives the Australian silky terrier an alert and lively appearance, in keeping with her temperament. A friendly dog, the Australian silky terrier is quite at home as part of a modern household. Although she is affectionate towards all her human family, the silky usually forms a particularly strong bond with one person.

Tenterfield Terrier

The Tenterfield terrier was only officially recognised by the Australian National Kennel Council in 2002. The breed name honours the Tenterfield saddler George Woolnough who was a well-known breeder of these hardy little dogs. Despite this relatively recent acknowledgement, the breed's origins can be traced back to the terriers arriving in Australia in the early 1800s, and before that to the now-extinct old English white terrier. Early arrivals were all shapes and sizes and with a variety of coats, but appearance didn't matter as long as the dog was good at doing its job: killing rats and other vermin.

Over the decades, this short-coated dog became established in Australia both as a means of pest control

A champion Tenterfield terrier at a Sporting Terrier Club of Victoria show in 2011.

A man and his Murray River retriever, proud owners of a cottage at Hill End, NSW, c.1872.

and as a companion, and it is believed it was bred quite extensively in northern New South Wales. For many years these dogs were known as miniature fox terriers, and in the early 1990s various clubs (in South Australia, Western Australia and New South Wales) joined together to establish a breed registry. However, it quickly became apparent that if the breed was to have a solid future, it needed a new name. 'Miniature fox terrier' suggested a smaller version of the well-known British breed, the smooth fox terrier, and this was definitely not the case. Owners took part in a ballot and overwhelmingly voted in favour of the name Tenterfield terrier.

Tenterfield terriers are compact, well-proportioned dogs; in fact, the breed standard specifies that 'the measurement of wither to ground and wither to rear point of buttock should be of equal proportions'. The coat is always short and smooth and colouring should be predominantly white with black, blue, tan or liver markings of any shade; a solid colour is not acceptable. The ideal Tenterfield is about 28 centimetres tall (although a range of 25.5 to 30.5 centimetres is allowed) and weight should be in proportion to height. A confident, intelligent dog, the Tenterfield terrier is bold and fearless when working, but a loving and loyal companion in the home.

Murray River Retriever

The Murray River retriever is perhaps the least known of the Australian breeds. The only retriever developed in Australia, the breed was officially recognised by the Australian National Kennel Council as a purebred gundog in 2022.

Genetic analysis clearly indicates that the Murray River retriever is a distinct breed,[7] although it can be grouped with other working and retrieving gundogs. Details of the Murray's early history have been largely lost, but it is believed retrievers of this type have been used in Australia since the early nineteenth century. As with all dog types, early breeders would only have been interested in a dog's ability to perform the required task; appearance would not have been important. By the 1890s, Murray River retrievers were breeding true to type and being used as game-retrieving dogs, particularly along the Murray River. The dog pictured at right appears almost identical to the Murray River retrievers of today.

The Murray's most distinguishing feature is her curly coat. The medium to tight curls are strongly textured and sit close to the skin, providing some water resistance as well as protection from harsh scrub when retrieving on land. Curls cover the entire body, except for the face, legs and paws, where the fur is smooth. Murrays are always solid liver in colour, although a white patch on the chest is sometimes seen. Standing somewhere between 46 and 53 centimetres at the shoulder, the Murray is considerably smaller than a Labrador retriever or a curly coated retriever. With a slightly rectangular body, strong tail flowing smoothly from the topline and powerful hindquarters, the Murray River retriever is clearly built for purpose. The face is framed by dropped (floppy) ears, and eyes vary in colour from amber to light brown.

Intelligent, friendly and confident, the Murray is loyal and loving towards her human family and makes a good companion, ready to play fetch or participate in agility, obedience or any other canine pursuit. She is energetic, a strong swimmer and a good retriever. With plenty of stamina and focus, the Murray River retriever is a highly trainable companion.[8]

A Murray River retriever sitting on a turnstile, South Australia, 1936.

CHAPTER 5

Australia's Antarctic Huskies

Sled dogs on board the *Southern Cross* prior to leaving for Antarctica, Hobart, 1898.

The Inuit people of the Arctic have used dogs to haul sledges and help with hunting for more than 1,000 years. In 1577 Englishman Martin Frobisher, in search of the Northwest Passage, reported that the Inuit:

> *Keep certain dogs, not much unlike wolves, which they yoke together, as we do oxen and horses, to a sled or trail, and so carry their necessaries over the ice and snow, from place to place.*[1]

Despite this evidence of the usefulness and suitability of Inuit-owned dogs in these conditions, European explorers in the Arctic did not use dog teams until 1820 (during a British naval expedition under the command of William Parry). After this, it was still over 30 years before it became the norm for Arctic explorers to use sledges and dogs. By the time explorers set their sights on Antarctica and the South Pole, there was a precedent for using the dogs commonly referred to as huskies to assist with travel and hauling in the extreme polar environment.

Antarctica was first sighted in 1820, and the following year Captain John Davis reported landing on the continent itself. Over 70 years later Carsten Borchgrevink, travelling as a deck hand with the whaling ship *Antarctic*, claimed the honour of being the first verified person to set foot on the Antarctic continent when a landing was made at Cape Adare on 24 January 1895. Borchgrevink was born in Norway but had emigrated to Australia in 1888. After his first trip to Antarctica, he returned to Australia keen to raise money for an expedition, but it took several years before he secured the financial backing he needed. When the expedition finally got under way, Borchgrevink took with him between 70 and 90 huskies (of Siberian and Greenland origin) and a crew of 31 men, including two dog handlers: Persen Savio and Ole Must.

Borchgrevink's ship, the *Southern Cross,* left London in August 1898 and docked in Hobart, Tasmania, in November. The colony's official photographer, John Watt Beattie, recorded the historic event, and among his photographs were several pictures of the dogs.

Leaving Hobart in December, Borchgrevink's expedition party reached Antarctica and set up a base at Cape Adare the following February. This was the first time dogs had set foot on Antarctica, and their presence would prove invaluable for decades to come. Two huts were built as preparations were made for a group to winter in Antarctica. It was far more difficult than anticipated, but in 1899, the shore party of ten men and 75 dogs spent winter at Cape Adare with only one human death. Although they did little more than exist, Borchgrevink and his expedition members proved it could be done. Their achievement inspired a number of polar explorers to set their sights on Antarctica.

Early explorers, from Captain Robert Falcon Scott in 1902 to Australian Douglas Mawson in 1912, all took huskies on their Antarctic expeditions with varying degrees of success.

Mawson's Australasian Antarctic Expedition of 1911–1914 can claim many achievements, particularly advancing scientific knowledge of Antarctica and charting large sections of the east Antarctic coastline. Despite great misfortune and tragedy, it marks the beginning of Australia's long and successful presence in the Antarctic. A large part of that success, at least in the first half of the twentieth century, can be attributed to the unflagging work of successive generations of huskies.

Exploring Antarctica would have been impossible without the strength and intelligence of dogs such as Shakespeare, photographed by Frank Hurley in 1914.

Aboard the *Commandant Charcot*. Dogs from this French expedition gave rise to Australia's Antarctic husky dynasty.

Beginnings of the Canine Dynasty

When we think of dogs associated with the Arctic and Antarctic, most people picture the types of dogs known throughout Australia today: the Alaskan malamute, believed to have originated with the Inupiaq people of Alaska; the Siberian husky, a lighter breed arising from dogs bred by the Chukchi people of northern Siberia; and even the Samoyed, a smaller white dog developed by the Samoyed people of eastern Siberia. But there are also several lesser-known breeds: in particular the Canadian husky, the genetically identical Greenland dog, and the Labrador husky. It was a mix of Greenland and Labrador huskies that founded the Australian Antarctic canine dynasty.

The Labrador husky breed—not to be confused with the Labrador retriever—originated in Canada's Labrador province, and its ancestors are believed to have arrived in that region with the Thule people (ancestors of the Inuit) around 1300 AD. Although originally quite closely related to other northern spitz types (such as Greenland and Siberian huskies), these dogs developed into an independent breed due to the isolation of this region of Canada.

The dogs that would ultimately give rise to generations of 'Australian' huskies were obtained from the French. In November 1948, the French expedition ship *Commandant Charcot* set sail from Cherbourg, France, on a mission to establish the first permanent French Antarctic station at Adélie Land, Antarctica. On board were 30 Labrador and Greenland huskies. But in the summer of 1948–1949, the pack ice off Adélie Land in the eastern Antarctic was impenetrable, and by February 1949, the ship was forced to retreat without reaching solid land. The commander of the expedition, André-Frank Liotard, didn't want to subject the dogs to the long sea voyage back to Europe, so he sent a message to Douglas Mawson at the University of Adelaide asking for assistance: could the huskies stay in Australia during the coming winter? After significant political wrangling, it was agreed that the huskies could be temporarily housed at Melbourne Zoo, using Monkey Island as a makeshift quarantine area. As part of the arrangement, it was agreed that any dogs born during that time, plus any dogs the French didn't want, would become Australia's property. Several litters were whelped, resulting in 22 puppies, and when the *Commandant Charcot* left Melbourne in December 1949, Australia had the beginnings of its own husky dynasty.

The French believed a cross of the Labrador and Greenland husky types produced the best working dogs. While the Greenland dogs had the best temperament and a short, thick coat, the Labrador huskies had a heavier build and greater strength. The temperaments of the different types were outlined in notes for Melbourne Zoo. The Labrador huskies were:

> *Very aristocratic dogs: in general capricious and nervous, more difficult to live with than the Greenlands. Family spirit is little developed. They will obey the strongest law. Feeble or timid dogs ought to be watched closely, and isolated if need be because they will be killed sooner or later by the others.*

By comparison, the Greenland dogs were considered to be:

> *Good dogs, rough and sober. Family spirit very well developed. They arrange their affairs among themselves and require less supervision than the Labradors.*[2]

Both types formed part of Australia's foundation group of huskies trained for use in Antarctica. Zoo staff had looked after the dogs well, but with only a small area available to them, the huskies were not active enough. The dogs would be crucial as a means of transport when Australia established permanent stations on the Antarctic continent, so it was vital they be fit and ready. In January 1950 a group of huskies was loaded aboard HMAS *Labuan*, destined for Heard Island, Australia's sub-Antarctic station in the Southern Ocean. Twelve dogs made this trip: ten Australian-born huskies and two older, experienced dogs from the original French group. They were: Buster and Trevor (the two Greenland-born dogs), Harbottle, Zoe, Thurber, Sheila, Pat, Willi, Boopus, Martan, Judy (actually born at sea just before arriving in Melbourne) and Phil.[3]

A careful breeding program was initiated on Heard Island—designed to retain the best features of both husky types—and a litter of nine puppies was born in September 1950, with an additional group of 16 huskies sent from Australia the following year.[4]

Just as importantly, the dogs were put into training: pulling sleds in winter and wheeled 'dogmobiles' in summer. This regimen not only got the huskies fit and used to working together in teams, it also proved valuable for Australian expeditioners, who gained experience in dog team management as well as developing routines which could be applied when they eventually travelled to Antarctica.

Finally, in January 1954, 30 huskies left Heard Island on the MV *Kista Dan,* bound for Mawson Station: Australia's first permanent base in Antarctica since Mawson's expedition of 1911–1914. In 1955, these original dogs were joined by another 15 huskies, and Australia also provided New Zealand with 28 dogs, helping that country establish its own husky population in Antarctica. In 1961, New Zealand returned the favour providing two pups, Terry and Colette, from its colony at Scott Base. With the addition of other dogs—including three Greenland huskies shipped directly from Greenland in 1963—the bloodline of Australia's dogs in Antarctica continued to strengthen and improve throughout the years.

The dogs proved vital to Australia's work and research in Antarctica. Some were ultimately transferred to two other Australian stations: Davis and Wilkes. The now-abandoned Wilkes, originally operated by the United States of America, was the predecessor of Australia's Casey Station.[5] When the Americans left the station for the last time, they left behind some malamute-type huskies, entrusting them to Australian care. These were large,

A team of eight huskies resting during a sledging run, 1950s.

strong dogs, but their individualistic nature made them less suited to teamwork. However, with careful crossbreeding with some of the Mawson huskies (by now closer to the Greenland type), the group of dogs continued to work well at Wilkes. In 1969, Wilkes was closed and the Australians made the permanent move to Casey Station, where the use of dogs continued until 1970. As the last huskies had left Davis Station in 1965, the cessation of dog operations at Casey meant Mawson Station was now the only home for Australia's dogs in Antarctica.

Huskies continued to work at Mawson for many more years. Dogs proved to be far safer and more reliable than any other form of transport such as snowmobiles, particularly on sea ice or crevassed plateau ice. Handlers, always attentive to their dogs' behaviour, could see when the huskies became anxious or started to step more carefully, a sign that the surface ahead could be dangerous. Dogs were also considered more reliable than motorised transport (which had a tendency to break down under harsh conditions); they created little or no pollution; and—while a balanced diet was preferred—in an extreme emergency huskies could be fed entirely 'off the land' on seal meat. In addition to all these benefits, huskies were great for the morale of Australians stationed in Antarctica.

However, huskies had some disadvantages. Travelling by dog sledge was slower than a snowmobile; and regardless of whether the dogs were working or idle, they had to be cared for and their training maintained constantly—the quality of the huskies' work depended on the amount of time a dog handler invested in them. Ultimately, it was the fact that huskies were an introduced species in a delicate ecosystem that proved to be the greatest drawback to their continued presence in Antarctica.

Checking weight and condition ahead of the final husky run, 1993.

Huskies like George worked hard and also provided emotional support to Australians in Antarctica.

Huskies in Training

In photographs, Australia's Antarctic huskies have a distinctive appearance. The ideal dog weighed just over 40 kilograms and measured about 60 centimetres at the shoulder. The coat could be black, white, tan, brown, buff or any combination of those colours, and consisted of an insulating felt beneath guard hairs. While the felt kept the dog warm, it was the guard hairs that protected the coat from being saturated by soft snow. A coat that was too long and shaggy—a problem with the original Labrador husky type—was a risk. Dogs with this sort of fur were prone to becoming encased in ice when resting and could seriously injure themselves when trying to tear free.

Provided the dogs had snow to burrow into, they were able to maintain body warmth in extreme weather. In blizzard conditions, huskies allowed the snow to bury them, providing shelter from the wind. However it was important that dogs didn't become completely buried and suffocate, so dog handlers always kept an eye on their charges. Staff at Australian Antarctic stations found that the huskies were quite comfortable in temperatures down to minus 48 degrees Celsius, but anything lower and 'they downed paws, went on strike, and refused absolutely to work'.[6]

Dogs performing hard work in such an extreme environment naturally needed a good diet. In the early days of Antarctic exploration, the huskies were mostly fed on seal meat cut into large chunks. In winter, dogs were fed a three-kilogram lump every two days, with a smaller ration in summer. By the 1940s, dogs were being fed compressed blocks of highly concentrated, energy-dense food called pemmican. Over the decades, their diet continued to be refined to provide optimum nutrition but one thing never changed: just like many pet dogs in Australia, the huskies' meals were often supplemented by kitchen scraps.

The huskies at Mawson were trained to respond to a basic set of commands, the most important being 'down' (or 'sit'). This settled the dogs when they were in harness, whether waiting for the command to go or pausing while the handler assessed the ground ahead.

Other commands included:

- 'Ready boys' – to get the team on their feet and ready to go;
- 'Mush' – spoken in a sharp, strong tone to get the team going;
- 'Left' – to turn left, said in a long, drawn-out tone and repeated to continue the turn;
- 'Right' – said in a short, sharp way to turn right; and
- 'Whoa' – spoken in a drawn-out, low tone to bring the team to a stop.[7]

These commands changed during the five decades huskies were working at the Australian Antarctic bases. Reports on the dogs from the 1950s mentioned that some of the dogs worked better if a handler used a French accent. It also seems that novice dog handlers (even those with experience of other dog breeds) found themselves struggling at times to manage the intelligent and headstrong huskies. For example, the 1954 dog report identified two commands for stopping: 'whoo' said quietly was for a normal stop, while 'whoo' spoken in an angry voice meant stop now or some dog is going to get in trouble! Regarding the angry-voice version, the report then went on to say, 'instead of stopping it usually has the reverse effect as all the dogs seem to have a guilty conscience'.[8] The report from 1962 noted that in order to be effective, the commands for left and right had to be given at just the correct moment, 'when the team thought it was time to change direction, otherwise all the shouting and pointing was of little avail'.[9] Despite these training problems, the reports also stated that without the skill and hard work of the dogs, the field program—at least in the early decades—would not have been possible.

The huskies' pulling power could be affected by many things—including temperature, surface conditions, fitness and mental stamina—but their work output was incredible. On flat ground and in reasonable snow and ice conditions, the Australian Antarctic huskies were each capable of pulling their own weight at a speed of five to six kilometres per hour. At slower speed, they could pull twice their own weight.

A good team could pull a fully laden sledge weighing several hundred kilograms for hours each day, with only five-minute breaks every half hour or hour. The 1954 report from Mawson stated that across the season, the main dog team (there were two full teams and a number of spare dogs that year) had travelled 1,931 kilometres and that both teams were capable of travelling about 40 kilometres each day when pulling a 318-kilogram sledge.[10]

The Never-forgotten Antarctic Huskies

Huskies proved to be an invaluable part of Australia's work in Antarctica, valued for their speed and ability to traverse almost any terrain. It's estimated that, over the years, Australian expeditions and scientists worked with nearly 1,000 dogs. Initially the dogs facilitated a significant amount of exploratory work along the coast, and into the mountains west and south of Mawson. As the Australian presence in Antarctica grew, the huskies were there every step of the way. At the end of the 1975–1976 summer, Mawson Station had 22 working dogs and some pups, and it looked as though the dogs were there to stay.

By 1988, Australia still had 26 huskies at Mawson, 18 of which made up two working teams. But the dogs' place in Antarctica was under threat: only Australia, Great Britain and Argentina were still using husky teams rather than relying entirely on motorised transport.

In 1991, the Madrid Protocol banned all non-native animals (besides humans) from Antarctica. The fight was on to try to save the huskies: Australia's living Antarctic heritage. What concerned the huskies' supporters most was that the protocol called for the dogs' 'removal'. Many people believed the huskies would be quietly destroyed, so nothing could be done to preserve their role in Antarctica.

The last husky run prior to leaving Antarctica for good, 1993.

Geologist and photographer Andrew Watson shared responsibility for the huskies' care, c.1912.

Public attention forced the Australian government to declare that the dogs would not be destroyed. Various action groups, including the 'Friends of the Polar Sledge Dogs' and the 'Keep Our Husky Heritage Alive Task Force' tried to convince the government that Australian citizens wanted the huskies to remain in Antarctica. By this stage, it was not even a question of continuing husky operations in the future, it was simply a case of allowing the remaining dogs to live out their days in the only environment they had ever known. But the Australian government was adamant: the huskies had to go.

The huskies' supporters then tried to ensure all the dogs would at least find suitable homes in Australia, but arrangements had already been made for 22 dogs to be sent to Minnesota in the United States. In their new home, there would be snow for six months of the year, the huskies would remain together and, importantly, they would still be doing the work they loved: pulling sledges. After the harsh living conditions and often extremely heavy workload of Antarctica, the huskies would find life in Minnesota luxurious by comparison.

A group of huskies was removed from Mawson during the summer of 1992. Their journey to the United States began on 4 November with a final run of the dogs from Mawson Station to the ship, RSV *Aurora Australis,* anchored 65 kilometres away at the edge of the sea ice. But with about 15 kilometres still to go, surface conditions had deteriorated and the huskies were helicoptered the final stretch to the ship. Before long, the dogs were sailing for Hobart. The huskies' departure marked the end of an incredible example of working relationships between people and dogs.

The Mawson huskies were accompanied by two of their handlers all the way to Ely, Minnesota. Within hours of their arrival, a team was harnessed and back in action. The Australian handlers remained in Minnesota throughout the winter, ensuring the huskies settled in properly and their new caretakers understood each dog's personality and how to work with these very special animals. The following year, five of these Mawson huskies—Jedda, Oscar, Merlin, Cocoa and Goohaw—were part of an expedition to the North Pole.

Not all the Mawson huskies were sent to the United States. Six older males—Ursa, Welf, Morrie, Elwood, Brendan and Bonza—remained behind. It was impossible for them to live out their years at Mawson and, in 1993, the last huskies left at the station were retired to Australia. Their paw prints are preserved on the plinth of an antenna mast at Mawson, a plaque recording their place in Australian Antarctic history. These last huskies arrived in Hobart in December and were homed with former Australian Antarctic expeditioners: people who knew the dogs and their needs. Because of their close bond, Morrie and Ursa were kept together, and made a number of public appearances in their new roles as retired canine heroes of Antarctica.

Although huskies no longer live and work in Antarctica, they have not been forgotten. Misty was only a few months old when she left Antarctica in 1993. One of the last litter to be born at Mawson, Misty spent her working life in the United States, retiring in 2003 and passing away in 2007. In 2011, some of Misty's ashes were brought 'home' to Mawson, incorporated into a plaque and small memorial mounted in the Dog Room, which houses memorabilia and photographs relating to the years of living and working with huskies at Mawson Station. The memorial is not just for Misty, the last of the Mawson huskies, but for all the huskies who served with Australians in Antarctica. Additionally, 26 landmarks near Mawson's base at Cape Denison—including Lassesen Island, Devil Rock and Ginger Reef—have been named after some of the intrepid huskies who served alongside Mawson and his men: a fitting tribute not only to the individual dogs, but to all the noble huskies who made Antarctic exploration possible.[11]

The huskies became quite accustomed to the local wildlife in Antarctica.

CHAPTER 6

Mascots

A painting of NSW Bushie, 'the celebrated Australian War dog'.

Animals have been involved in human wars for millennia. Images from the ancient world show fighting dogs accompanying warriors, and there are accounts of Greek soldiers heading into battle accompanied by large, fierce dogs. The Romans were known to use dogs as messengers and as guards of cities and military camps, and dogs are frequently depicted in battle scenes in ancient Egyptian art.[1] Just as dogs in the ancient world were often kept as pets and beloved companions, there is also evidence that soldiers going off to battle sought comfort from their canine friends. One author notes that in ancient Greek art dating to around the fifth century BC, it is common to see scenes where a dog bids his master farewell as the armed warrior sets off to war.[2]

It is not clear when soldiers first began adopting animal mascots and taking them to war, but the practice has a very long history. One of the best-known mascots from centuries past is Boye, the white poodle belonging to Prince Rupert, Count Palatine of the Rhine. Prince Rupert was the nephew of Charles I of England and first cousin of King Charles II of England. Rupert had proven himself in battle from a young age. Boye (actually a female) was a gift from the English Earl of Arundel and she became Prince Rupert's constant companion, whether on the battlefield or at the royal courts. As a commander of cavalry for royalist forces during the English Civil War (1642–1651), Rupert also became a prominent figure in propaganda, and that meant Boye did too.

Wild stories suggested Boye had magical powers, was a dog-witch or could catch a bullet aimed at her master in her mouth.[3] Magic aside, Boye was loved by the royalist soldiers and given the rank of sergeant major general. It may be that Boye's supposed powers are part of the reason animal mascots are sometimes considered to be lucky charms.

From this point on it appears canine mascots became, if not exactly common, then a more prominent part of military life. One of the earliest known images of a British canine mascot is an unsigned painting in the National Army Museum, United Kingdom, titled *The 25th Regiment of Foot in Minorca (Menorca).*[4] It dates to c.1771 and shows a group of redcoats accompanied by a pug dog. The first documented regimental mascot was a goat. The Royal Welch Fusiliers adopted a goat during a 1775 battle in the American War of Independence, and a goat has served with the regiment ever since.

Possibly one of the most famous Australian mascots was a dog named Horrie, companion to the men of the 2/1st Machine Gun Battalion during World War II. However, Australia's first canine mascots appear to have been the dogs who travelled with troops bound for South Africa and the Boer War (1899–1902). Contingents of soldiers from both Victoria and New South Wales were accompanied by canine mascots. Two of the dogs were collie-type working dogs, and both were named Bushie: New South Wales' Bushie was the New South Wales Citizens' Bushmen's mascot. Together with Nelson, the official South Australian mascot, they were the first dogs to have documented associations with the Australian armed forces.

In addition to the official mascots, reports indicate that quite a large number of dogs and other animals made the trip to South Africa. According to Reverend James Green, who travelled aboard the ship SS *Maplemore,* a possum and two other dogs joined New South Wales' Bushie on the journey from Sydney; and another six dogs were brought on board with the South Australian troops.[5] The departing troops were informed that as authorities in Cape Town would not allow the

Australia's most famous canine mascot, Horrie the war dog.

Sergeant Matthew Morey's dog, Bushie, with members of the 3rd Victorian Bushmen Contingent in South Africa.

dogs to land, all animals would be put ashore in Fremantle, Western Australia. Despite this, soldiers embarking from Fremantle actually brought more dogs on board. However, when it was time to depart and the order came to 'dismiss dogs', there was not a dog to be found; that is, until the ship got past Rottnest Island and out to sea, when a number of dogs reappeared. Ultimately, as the ship did not make port in Cape Town, the dogs successfully landed elsewhere in South Africa with their human companions.

New South Wales' Bushie had joined the NSW Citizens' Bushmen's Contingent thanks to the Animal Protection Society. Recognising the mutual affection between a bushman and his dog, the society decided to present the departing troops with a contingent dog.[6] This is significant because it shows that in 1900, the public and press acknowledged the emotional connection shared between humans and dogs. The decision to present the troops with a dog indicates a wider awareness of the importance of the human–animal bond and the comfort a dog can bring, particularly in situations that cause humans stress.

Lieutenant-governor Sir Frederick Darley christened New South Wales' Bushie, and one soldier, Trooper Battye, was specifically assigned to care for the dog.[7] At the end of the war, Bushie was presented to Queen Victoria; after his humble beginnings in a cottage at Wentworth Falls, New South Wales, Bushie enjoyed a privileged retirement at the royal kennels.[8]

Victoria's Bushie belonged to Sergeant Matthew Morey. Morey had been a constable in the Victoria Mounted Police Force but resigned to volunteer for South Africa and was given the dog by a police colleague. According to newspaper accounts, Victoria's Bushie had a tough time of it. On the ship, he was stabbed by a sailor but recovered from his severe wound and was able to land with the contingent. On the road in South Africa, Bushie was infested with ticks and lost the use of his hind legs, but Morey refused to abandon his companion. Instead, Bushie rode on a baggage wagon for three weeks until he recovered.

A fundraising photo of Nelson, mascot of the South Australian Bushmen Contingent.

Bushie was lost at one point during fighting. Fortunately he was wearing a miniature saddle inscribed with his name and regiment. He was adopted by Scottish soldiers, remaining with them until he was captured by the Boers. He managed to escape, and travelled more than 240 kilometres to rejoin the Scottish regiment. The Boers caught him again, but once again he escaped and made his way back to the Scottish regiment. Finally, when the Victorian Bushmen's Contingent combined forces with Scottish troops, Bushie was reunited to his astonished owner. During his time away from the Victorians Bushie had been shot in the chest (and possibly through the tongue), but once again recovered from his wounds.[9] He returned to Australia with his regiment, arriving in Victoria on 6 June 1901; but Bushie's work wasn't done.

While most of his time was spent in comfortable semi-retirement in Toorak, Bushie was also taken to various dog shows in Melbourne wearing a small barrel around his neck to raise money for the Children's Hospital.

Nelson, a Newfoundland from South Australia, was another Boer War dog. He was held in such high regard that his portrait was painted.[10] Technically he was the first official canine mascot, beating the two Bushies by a few months. The media initially referred to Nelson as a Saint Bernard (even, on several occasions, as a 'prize Saint Bernard') and it seems that only after his return from South Africa was he identified as a Newfoundland. Photographs confirm this is correct. The confusion is understandable, as Newfoundlands were used to revive the Saint Bernard breed during the 1850s, and so for many years the breeds appeared very similar.

Nelson is an important example of a military mascot's role. He was clearly beloved and a great morale booster both for the men of the South Australian contingent, and for the various regiments—both British and South African—that he encountered along the way. Following Nelson's return from war, he also found favour with the Australian public. His war exploits were widely reported and Nelson was taken on tour (together with a horse named Bugler)[11] to raise funds for a National Memorial in Adelaide. The memorial was to be an equestrian statue 'commemorative of the part taken by soldiers of [South Australia] in the task of consolidating the Empire'.[12] Accompanied by two returned soldiers who delivered a presentation on the war, Bugler and Nelson spent many months touring regional South Australia. At each venue, Nelson was fitted with his collecting panniers and handed into local children's care to do the rounds. Nelson also had some tricks that enlivened presentations and no doubt helped the fundraising. For example, when the presenting returned soldier said 'Boers, Nelson!' the dog—from his position on stage—would immediately emit two or three deep bays, to the delight of the crowd.[13] Additional funds were raised by selling photographs of Nelson and Bugler (at left).

An article in *The Northern Argus* reveals just how good Nelson and Bugler were at opening a crowd's hearts and wallets in the small town of Auburn, South Australia. It states that Nelson's collecting box brought in '10s 6d from the children of the State school' while photograph sales raised the total to £6 14s 6d.[14] It is indicative of the Australian regard for animals that a dog and a horse were instrumental in raising thousands of pounds towards the commissioning of an equestrian statue from one of Britain's foremost animal sculptors of the day.[15]

Not Just Dogs

During World War I, 'cats, possums, wallabies, kangaroos, dogs (bulldogs, sheepdogs and other breeds), monkeys, birds, pigs, donkeys, white rabbits ... all made the trip to Gallipoli or Europe'.[16] While it has been stated that these mascots were important for fun, raising spirits and as good luck charms, it is also important to consider the strong emotional bonds between soldiers and the animals who accompanied them. The lengths taken to smuggle many of these animals on board troop ships, and keep them hidden during inspections and safe on the battlefield, indicate a far greater emotional investment than would be expected for a mere fun diversion. These animals were the soldiers' close companions; and, unsurprisingly, canine mascots were dearly cherished.

Mascots, whether official or unofficial, have a very important part to play when soldiers go to war. Unlike dogs with jobs—guard dogs, messengers, explosives detection dogs and so on—mascots aren't necessarily highly trained, but they're often unsung heroes. Many canine mascots warned their soldier companions of danger, and all helped the men in different ways. Those dogs who travelled with troops from Australia were a reminder of home and what was waiting when the servicemen and women returned. Obviously an emotional connection between soldier and dog

Staff Sergeant Boris leads the 13th Infantry Battalion through Katoomba on a trek from Ingleburn camp to Bathurst, NSW, 1940.

During the Second World War, Blue was the only dog permitted access to Victoria Barracks, Brisbane, and wore a special collar proving his identity.

would be greatest for an individual who managed to take his beloved pet to a distant battlefield, but the benefits of a canine mascot were also there for all the other servicemen and women in the dog's vicinity. In the same way, a dog picked up along the way, or a stray who had simply become attached to a group of Australian soldiers, became just as important as the dogs that were Australian-born.

Canine mascots provided hope, companionship, laughter, sympathy, affection and unquestioning love to men and women engaged in the serious and often horrifying business of war, thousands of kilometres away from their human loved ones. Having a dog to care for amid death and destruction, a non-judgemental companion with whom to share fears and even tears—emotions that couldn't necessarily be expressed between 'tough' soldiers—gave soldiers hope and boosted morale. A dog who could perform a few tricks would keep men entertained and take their minds off where they were, even if only for a moment. Having a mascot helped soldiers get through the difficulty of adjusting to military life and carried them through the days and weeks when war surrounded them and home seemed like a distant memory.

Mascots inspired pride among the soldiers, often wearing some item that identified their country or particular military unit. Victoria's Bushie had a saddle inscribed with that information, and sailors' hats for navy dogs or a coat with the relevant colours of a country or military unit were also common. Many mascots were considered to be good luck charms. In fact, the *Macquarie Dictionary* defines mascot as 'a person, animal, or thing supposedly bringing good luck', and the word derives from *masco*, an old French Provençal word meaning 'witch'. The type or breed of mascot could symbolise courage and fighting spirit, or be an indication of the place of origin of a particular military unit. For many Australian soldiers, this meant a kangaroo mascot, but in World War I in particular, Australia's strong ties to Great Britain meant the British bulldog was a popular choice.

Even before the outbreak of World War I, the bulldog was firmly associated with British courage and determination, making it an obvious choice for soldiers serving with Britain and her allies. As part of the British Empire, Australian soldiers were quick to adopt the British bulldog as a suitable mascot. A search through Australian newspapers of the World War I era shows just how popular the British bulldog was with Australian troops. The breed was favoured to boost morale, stir up Australia's patriotic feelings towards the mother country and champion the Allied cause, both on the home front and in the field. There was Colonel Stone, mascot of the 42nd Battalion; the 10th Battalion's Bill; Australia Bill, with the 38th Battalion's A Company; Digger, briefly the Australian Army Reserve Band's mascot (until he ran away); as well as numerous other British bulldogs belonging to a variety of different army units and navy crews.[17] In the Library's collections is a stereograph of soldiers of the Australian Naval and Military Expeditionary Force, taken at the army training camp at Broadmeadows in 1914; unsurprisingly, the mascot belonging to the men of B Company, 7th Battalion Infantry was another bulldog, named Bill.[18]

The popularity of the British bulldog as a mascot among the Australian military continued through to World War II, where the likes of Warspite, Buller Churchill, Roger, Bill and Digger kept morale high and stirred up Australian crowds when they marched on parade.[19]

According to a message written in June 1916, Tassie, the mascot of Tasmania's Fighting 40th Battalion, was given to the soldiers by a Mr Butler of Hobart. The purebred British bulldog, admired both for his fierce looks and docile nature, was considered to be Tasmania's dog. He was cared for by Sergeant John Reid Wilson,[20] and quickly became a great favourite with all the men. Before Tassie went away to war, the men trained him to march by himself in front of a military band. Apparently his presence added 'considerable interest' to parades.[21] Of course, there were also dogs of many other

Quarter Master Sergeant William Carroll and his mate at Broadmeadows Army camp, c.1916.

breeds supporting the troops, from kelpies and German shepherds to small terriers and mixed breeds. Every one of them was the pride of their particular unit or ship.

Mascots in Pictures

As well as formal and media photographs of mascots, it is not uncommon to find pictures of soldiers with their beloved pet dogs, taken in the days or weeks before they left Australian shores. Naturally, their proud relatives wanted a picture of the young man in uniform, and by choosing to include his dog in the picture, each of those soldiers was showing just how much he cared about his dog. It not only meant the soldier had a picture of his dog that could be carried into battle—just as some young men might have a picture of their wife, girlfriend or other significant person—but it also said something about how those dog-loving young men saw themselves. By giving their loved ones a picture that included the dog, each man was effectively saying, 'this is how I want you to think of me'.

Regardless of whether dogs were official regimental mascots, companions smuggled aboard troop ships, adopted in the field or beloved pets left at home, each image including a dog is a testament to the importance of dogs in the soldiers' lives. It didn't matter whether a dog had arrived with one man or been adopted by an entire company or regiment. Official or unofficial, in a training camp or on the battlefield, a canine mascot quickly became important to everybody.

At the time there was no scientific evidence to back up the benefits of having a dog, but research has now proven that canine companionship is beneficial for mental as well as physical health. Scientific studies have not been carried out on soldiers during war, but have examined pet owners and people under stressful peacetime conditions. Using physiological signs of stress such as heart rate and blood pressure, scientists have consistently shown that the presence of a dog

The British bulldog was a popular choice as mascot for Australian soldiers during the First World War.

904. AN APPROPRIATE MASCOT the British Bulldog with the AUSTRALIAN EXPEDITIONARY FORCE at BROADMEADOWS. Copyright 1914 by Geo. Rose.
THE ROSE STEREOGRAPHS
MELBOURNE SYDNEY, WELLINGTON & LONDON.

can help to reduce stress.[22] In fact, the presence of a dog is even better than having a close friend around. It makes sense that the same benefits of dog companionship would be felt by soldiers in battle conditions, and there is plenty of anecdotal evidence to support this theory.[23]

The mascots and mates that accompanied Australian soldiers into war endured battles and suffered along with the men, their loyalty never wavering. During World War II, United States general Dwight D. Eisenhower perhaps explained it best when he spoke of how much a dog meant to men on the battlefield:

> *The friendship of a dog is precious. It becomes even more so when one is so far removed from home ... I have a Scottie. In him I find consolation and diversion ... he is the 'one person' to whom I can talk without the conversation coming back to the war.*[24]

There is little recognition for mascots, regardless of whether they were dogs, cats, kangaroos or an entirely different species, but their contribution to the war effort should not be overlooked or forgotten. A canine mascot may not seem as heroic as a trained messenger dog, dashing from the trenches with vital information about enemy positions; but to the soldiers whose days were made a little brighter by the affection of a four-legged mate, having a mascot was a blessing. These dogs and other animals may not have had official status or particular jobs, but their presence in the trenches and on the ships was just as important as that of any working animal. Staunch companions, beloved friends and reminders of normal life, these mascots provided the love and support that helped soldiers endure the horrors of war.

Even pretend soldiers need a loyal mascot, Canberra, 1958.

CHAPTER 7

Outback Dogs

A mounted policeman in the outback uses his hat as a dog (and horse) water bowl, c.1935.

In the first half of the twentieth century, the advent of motor cars and, ultimately, aeroplanes meant that outback Australia became far more accessible. Although stock routes, stations and townships had already encroached on land that for tens of thousands of years had been home only to Aboriginal people, there was now a new wave of people eager to travel across the outback or bring aid to those who called the remotest parts of Australia home. And very often, they took their dogs with them.

For people living in these parts of Australia, a dog chosen for her ability to guard or work stock could also become a firm friend; but when the objective was simply to travel from A to B by unconventional means, the decision to bring a dog on the trip could only arise from one thing: mateship. Not only did the men who set off on these outback adventures test new modes of transport, but they also took along cameras (sometimes even movie cameras) and documented their journeys for all to see. Trips that were initially undertaken simply to determine if they could be done became a way of showing urban Australians—and the rest of the world—the amazing country that existed beyond the fringes of civilisation. This chapter takes a dog-lover's view of a couple of those characters, their travels across the outback and, most importantly, their canine companions.

A photograph from 1913 (at right) of an unnamed dog on an outback expedition gives a hint of just how important dogs were to these intrepid adventurers. The image shows a small black-and-white dog perched across the front of a camel's saddle, looking quite at home. The dog was part of the group accompanying Captain Samuel Albert White on a trip to the Everard and Musgrave Ranges in Central Australia. White was an ornithologist and his journeys into the outback were for the purposes of collecting scientific specimens and completing a survey of the birds of South Australia and much of the Northern Territory. His most important work was his collaboration with Gregory Mathews on the 12-volume *The Birds of Australia*.[1] Taking a dog by camel into remote Australia in the hope of documenting bird species doesn't seem to be particularly logical; but then again, a dog's company can often outweigh any minor problems a canine presence may cause. Presumably the little dog had been trained not to bark or chase the birds!

Francis Birtles: A Dog Person

Francis (Frank) Birtles was born in Fitzroy, Melbourne in 1881 and it seemed he was always destined for a life of adventure. After time in the merchant navy, he honed his bushcraft skills in South Africa, becoming increasingly adept at self-sufficiency in a semi-arid environment. Birtles made his first great cycling trip in that country, travelling from Calvinia to Noupoort across the semi-desert Karoo region—but it would be his Australian adventures that would make Frank Birtles a household name.[2]

Birtles made his first Australian trip in 1906, peddling his bicycle from Fremantle in Western Australia across the Nullarbor to Melbourne, then on to Sydney—a journey of over 3,500 kilometres through some of Australia's harshest and loneliest country. He left Fremantle on 26 December 1906 and reached Sydney Town Hall 113 days later on 8 May 1907. To 'complete' the trip, he then cycled to Bondi and stood on the shore of the Pacific Ocean. Birtles wasn't the only adventurer pitting himself against remote Australia; there were other

A relaxed expedition mascot and a member of Captain White's party riding a camel in Central Australia, 1913.

Yowie waits for his share of dinner.

young men with bicycles and motor cars striving to break records or simply push themselves and their machines to the limit. What set Birtles apart was his ability to not only publicise himself and his travels, but to attract sponsors for his endeavours. A key part of that was the fact that from the very first trip, Birtles travelled with a camera. Later he would also take movie as well as still cameras, including all the attendant paraphernalia this equipment required in the early part of the twentieth century.

After several more bicycle trips, Birtles was ready for the next challenge: outback Australia by motor car. This not only opened up the possibility to new types of travel—faster, further, more remote—it also meant Birtles could travel with company, both human and canine.

By 1912, Frank Birtles was a celebrity. He claimed to have cycled across Australia six times in the previous six years, and his photographs and film brought the remotest parts of the outback to city audiences. His 1912 bicycling movie *Across Australia with Francis Birtles the Intrepid Overlander* was already a box office sensation when Birtles was approached by the Canada Cycle and Motor Company, the Australian agents for Brush motor cars. In a daring publicity stunt to promote the Brush, the company wanted Frank to accompany mechanic Syd Ferguson in a drive from Perth to Sydney. If they pulled it off, it would be the first time a motor car had made a latitudinal crossing of the continent—and given the basic nature of the Brush Runabout, it would also be a miracle. On their way to the departure point, Ferguson acquired Rex, a white dog with a black patch over one eye and all the enthusiasm for adventure you'd expect from a young terrier. Rex's chosen position on the heavily laden Brush was atop a blanket roll that had been lashed to a running board. Birtles and Ferguson fashioned a makeshift safety rail by lashing a sapling from the front mudguard to the rear, ensuring Rex wouldn't fall off. As Birtles reported after the successful journey, 'Rex made a doggy record by being the first to cross Australia from Fremantle W.A. to Sydney'.[3]

At journey's end, Rex seems to have remained with Ferguson, but he paved the way for many dogs to join Birtles on his future outback adventures.

Birtles was clearly a dog person. In later years he wrote of the dog he'd had as a child and the dingo pup he'd befriended when cycling across Australia. When one of his dogs died during a journey the tough bushman was almost brought to tears.[4] Birtles was well known for his ability to swear 'beyond the limits of ordinary profanity'; according to one journalist he could 'swear in Australianese, Aboriginalese, Chinese, Japanese, journalese, and best of all, in Birtle-ese'.[5] But all that changed when it came to his dogs. Then, this hard, sunburned man of the bush would turn to mush; he adored his dogs and they adored him back. So much did Birtles love his dogs that his 1935 book, *Battle Fronts of Outback,* was dedicated 'to Dinkum. A blue Australian cattle-dog, my sole companion on many a tough track in the great outback wilds of Australia'.[6] It wasn't long before his dogs became almost as famous as Frank himself as they accompanied him from one side of the country to the other.

Birtles' first famous dog was Wowser, a bulldog named because 'he looked on the world with such a fixed expression of disapproval'.[7] Wowser crossed Australia six times in Birtles' company and the two seemed to have had similar temperaments. Just like Birtles, Wowser never hesitated to throw himself headlong into a fray. On one occasion, dog and overlander encountered a fully laden camel train in the town of Menindee in the far west of New South Wales. According to Birtles, Wowser ambled over to introduce himself to a camel and was kicked for his trouble and bowled over several times. He responded by latching on to the camel's leg and refusing to let go. As Wowser and the camel spun about, the rest of the 50-strong camel train broke their lines and scattered with saddles, rations and blankets falling off in all directions. Although no animals seemed to have sustained serious damage, it 'was the greatest commotion [Menindee] had seen for many a day'.[8] Wowser apparently also liked to stir

Birtles' brother Clive and Wowser don their goggles, ready to hit the open road.

A tribute from the heart: 'Wowser, my chum across Australia 3 times'.

up trouble with other dogs met along the way, regardless of whether they were station dogs, Indigenous peoples' pets or a pack of wild dingoes. As one journalist said, Wowser 'simply applied the most ferocious part of his wrinkled countenance to the business in hand, and things generally came his way, except alligators and crocodiles'.[9]

Wowser was devoted to Birtles. He once saved him from an attacking wild boar, managing—despite being raked several times by the animal's tusks—to hold it at bay until Birtles was able to come to his dog's aid.[10] On another trip, this time between Birdsville, Queensland and the Gulf of Carpentaria, trouble with the car and difficult terrain reduced speed to a crawl and water supplies dipped perilously low before running out completely. Soon after the car broke down entirely, and Wowser and Birtles set off in search of the Georgina River. Wowser walked in his master's shadow, occasionally stumbling with heat and exhaustion. When they stopped to rest, Wowser would again crawl into Birtle's shadow and lie there gasping until it was time to move again. Birtles tried to carry his dog but was too weak to manage the task. They walked through the night and, at some point, Birtles noticed that Wowser seemed a little brighter: he was walking out in front, head up, scenting the air. Then a flock of ducks flew over them, low, clearly heading for water. They staggered on. Suddenly, Wowser gave a whine. Water! Once their thirst was slaked, there was still the problem of being stranded in the outback, so Birtles and Wowser followed the river upstream hoping to find a cattle station. A wire fence, hoof prints and then a homestead roof were signposts to salvation. Birtles and his dog were welcomed at the station and nursed back to health, with Wowser 'put on a diet of dainties'[11] until his strength was restored.

Outback exploits aside, it was often Wowser's photogenic qualities and behaviour in the city at journey's end that made him a crowd favourite. Newspapers reported that after three months in the Northern Territory and western Queensland with Birtles and cameraman Frank Hurley,

Wowser 'growled for joy' when he saw city people again.[12] That trip resulted in the movie *Into Australia's Unknown* (1915). Wowser clearly left a lasting impression on Birtles, and in years to come he would name other dogs after his first true companion of the outback.

Some of Birtles' dogs, like Chancer the bulldog, didn't get much press. The next canine to make a name for himself as part of Birtles' overlanding team was Dinkum—the dog immortalised in Birtles' dedication in *Battle Fronts of Outback*. Dinkum was a large Australian cattle dog who, legend has it, was born in a hollow log somewhere in Cape York. From that point on, Dinkum and Birtles were virtually inseparable.

Dinkum was a dog of many talents. In the middle of a busy city, he would guard the car (often wearing his enormous driving goggles), oblivious to the meat pies and other treats offered by the adoring public. Only if someone dared to touch the battered vehicle's chassis would he rouse, fixing the perpetrator with a cold, hard eye that clearly warned of more to come if necessary. Dinkum travelled across Australia several times by car and also made a couple of long outback treks with Birtles on foot. For his encounters with snakes, wild buffaloes and boars, Dinkum was awarded the Royal Humane Society's bravery medal. When he was shown film of himself doing battle, Dinkum had to be restrained from attacking the movie screen. For a time, Dinkum was also the most experienced flying canine in the country. He was the first dog to fly across the Blue Mountains in an aeroplane; he accompanied Birtles on a transcontinental flight and clocked up over 5,000 air miles (8,046 kilometres), as well as flying to the dizzying height of 12,000 feet (3,658 metres). The hero dog also had a bit of a weak spot—like many dogs—for a good meaty bone, and would collect them quite religiously. Should an aeroplane chance to fly overhead, Dinkum would be forced to hastily bury his stash. Such was Dinkum's fame that when Birtles had to travel to England, Lady Stonehaven, wife of the then governor-general of Australia, offered Dinkum accommodation at Government House: a life of luxury far from

Francis Birtles and Dinkum, equally at home on a camel's back as in the car, Heavitree Gap, Alice Springs, 1921.

Dinkum takes the wheel.

the dust of Australia's outback. Dinkum's fans also wrote him letters, which he 'answered' with tales of cars, aeroplanes and the outback adventures he'd shared with his human.[13]

Dinkum's heeler heritage came to the fore on one expedition when Birtles' car broke down in south-western Queensland. As Birtles was wondering how to fashion a replacement part out of odds and ends, Dinkum, clearly aware that the car was failing to do as it was told, took matters into his own paws. Leaping from his seat, Dinkum ran around behind the car and began nipping at the back tyres in an effort to get things moving again. He wasn't successful, but his efforts were greatly appreciated.

Dinkum also knew when the occasion called for calm and stealth. In June 1924, Birtles, Dinkum and Wowser rolled out of Sydney in a brand new Bean motor car.[14] The intent was to prove the British car's suitability for Australia's tough outback conditions. This time they had company: journalist Malcolm Ellis and Bean Cars engineer John Simpson. At one point during the journey, Ellis reported being woken by Dinkum's cold nose in the middle of his face. He pushed the dog away but Dinkum tried again, now adding two gentle paws. Ellis came fully awake, knowing something was wrong in camp—something that required a quiet warning. He looked about. Dinkum was lying next to him, staring hard at the end of Ellis' swag. At that moment, Ellis became aware of a cold weight across his ankles. There was a snake; possibly in the swag with him. Thanks to Dinkum, Ellis was able to leap clear of his blanket roll, which subsequently proved to contain a death adder. After it was all over and the snake removed some way from camp, 'Dinkum permitted himself the luxury of a growl'.[15]

On the same trip another of Dinkum's talents—this one a tribute both to his temperament and the bond he shared with Birtles—became evident to Birtles' travelling companions. During his time in Africa, Birtles had contracted malaria and also suffered from one of the disease's most dangerous complications: blackwater fever. Occasionally and without warning he would suffer a relapse, experiencing a high fever

December 1924: Birtles and Dinkum arrive in Sydney after driving an Oldsmobile Six from Darwin to Adelaide, in a record-breaking 9 days, 9 hours and 15 minutes.

and mental disturbances such as paranoia, fear and anger. As Birtles would begin to recover his senses, Dinkum would place a gentle paw on his arm and, according to Ellis, 'a few moments afterwards we would hear these two old comrades at their usual gentle, half intelligible dog talk about the game of the country-side'.[16]

Yowie the German shepherd was another of the dogs who accompanied Birtles into the country's interior. After a couple of short (for Birtles) trips, dog and man headed for the Northern Territory where they remained for 20 months. Depending on conditions, Yowie's diet included everything from insects and frogs to iguanas and crocodile, and (perhaps not surprisingly) he showed a definite liking for Birtles' damper. In December 1930, shortly after their return from the north, Birtles took Yowie along to the Alsatian Shepherd Dog Club of South Australia's show.[17] It seems an uncharacteristic move for a man accustomed to dirt and solitude to present his dog in the more rarefied atmosphere of the show ring, but perhaps it was simply another way for the overlander to promote his exploits. According to Birtles, wherever he went crowds flocked to see Yowie, the famous dog who had travelled over 22,530 kilometres throughout Australia. Thousands of people had offered to buy the handsome dog, but all offers were refused; Yowie was Birtles' staunch companion and 'far better company than most men'.[18]

It seems that throughout his life, Birtles was a man who captured the public's imagination, but he could be very difficult to deal with. No-one knows precisely how many times he crossed Australia; some reports say 70, some more. Although he had human company on many of his expeditions, he clearly preferred the companionship of his canine sidekicks. Without his faithful dogs it is doubtful Birtles would have survived many of his near misses deep in the Australian outback.

Yowie surveys the country, overlooking the railway line at Alice Springs, c.1929.

Eccerty keeps a sharp eye on proceedings as the Morris truck descends into a gully at Mount Dockrell, Western Australia.

Michael Terry's Canine Companions

Michael Terry was born in Gateshead, northern England in 1899. As a teenager during World War I he learnt to drive a car to help his mother with her war work, before joining the Royal Navy Air Service Armoured Car Section in 1917. Terry's lungs were damaged while on service and after his discharge, doctors advised him to move to a warmer climate. He decided to move to Australia, arriving in Fremantle on 31 January 1919.

Terry was an adventurer at heart, drawn to the vastness of Australia's outback. In 1923 he teamed up with Richard Yockney and the pair purchased a 1913 Model T Ford, which they heavily modified for bush conditions. From February to October of that year they drove from Winton, Queensland to Broome, Western Australia, a journey detailed in Terry's book *Across Unknown Australia.*[19] On this trip, the men were sadly without a dog for company.

Terry was enthusiastic about the prospect of opening up Australia with motor transport. Like Frank Birtles, Terry also understood the power of publicity. He became a prolific writer, documenting and photographing his various journeys; ultimately, he wrote about more than 14 trips across Australia's red heart between 1923 and 1935. While popular here, he was particularly well known in Britain, perhaps because his outback tales seemed far more adventurous to those not quite so familiar with the country. Terry wasn't an explorer: his motorised travel relied on stopping at stations, outposts and towns to stockpile fuel for the next leg of the journey. He was simply a man with a spirit of adventure and a passion for outback Australia.

In 1925 Terry travelled from Darwin to Broome with six other men: R.A. Prescott, C.F. 'Jock' Syme, E.E. 'Joker' Jolley, A.E. 'Elusive' Smitheram, M. Redknap and Lord Apsley. The group went by train from Darwin to Katherine where they began the expedition proper, making the rest of the trip in an A.J. Stevens motorcycle with sidecar and two Guy Roadless Vehicles with trailers.[20] Terry's party became the first group to travel part of the northern section of the Canning Stock Route in motorised vehicles—and they were accompanied for the entire journey by Girlie, a small black-and-white terrier. Syme had purchased Girlie in Brisbane and named her for her good looks.

Girlie was particularly devoted to Syme and always travelled in her own special place on the truck he drove. She proved to be very much a city dog and rather out of her depth in the bush. She would snuggle into bedrolls when the owner wasn't looking and would never lap from a waterhole, always sitting patiently and waiting for one of the men to offer her a drink from a tin dish. Girlie was much loved by all the men: they greatly enjoyed her company and were constantly entertained by her many antics. Each morning, Girlie would wake Syme by covering his face with licks, then proceed to scamper around the camp and wake each man in the same way, before finally rounding off the whole process with a series of joyous barks.

The men discovered early on that Girlie was quite gun shy. The first time they shot birds for food, Girlie leapt into the nearest car and was found cowering among the supplies. This was the case every time throughout the entire trip, except for a couple of occasions when she found herself too far from a car to hide. Then she simply bolted into the bush, and the last the adventurers saw of her for several hours was her black-and-white backside disappearing into the scrub. Chasing her was useless, so the men were left to an anxious wait, hoping Girlie would return without encountering a dingo or snake. Girlie did, however, turn out to be an excellent watchdog, quickly learning who belonged at camp—wherever that happened to be—and who did not. Strangers were met with snarls, bared teeth and a flurry of barks.

To gain her spot in the car, Girlie would take a leap onto the front tyre, another onto the footboards and a third onto the seat, then settle in among the packing cases where she was shaded by the canopy. From there, she would turn around and poke her head around the corner of the canopy,

Time to stretch! Eccerty has a dig and runs out ahead of the truck, Western Australia, 1928.

Bill and Spot share a tent on Terry's expedition, Western Australia, 1928.

just by Syme's right ear, where she could watch the passing land and catch the breeze. Keenly interested in the scenery, Girlie would let out a series of deafening barks if she spotted any cattle or if the branches of a tree brushed the vehicle canopy as they drove past, which must have been delightful for Syme! True to her terrier nature, Girlie found many things to bark at. She barked when chasing lizards or when the men were forced to kill a snake that had come too close to camp. When the travellers visited Lake Gregory in Western Australia—at that time surrounded by dry, salt-crusted flats after several years of drought—Girlie barked with delight at the salty air. And naturally, Girlie barked to alert the men to anything or anyone straying close to camp at night.

When passing through land surrounding Jubilee Downs Homestead near Fitzroy Crossing, the travellers were forced to open and close a number of gates. At one point, with the trucks sitting side by side, Girlie jumped into the wrong vehicle. She was lavished with pats to keep her quiet and it wasn't until they'd travelled several miles down the road that Syme realised she was missing. He brought his truck to an abrupt halt and was all set to race back to the last gate to collect poor Girlie. But the prank couldn't be sustained; Girlie gave the game away with her excited yapping and was quickly reunited with her master.

In 1928 Terry began another trip, this time from Port Hedland in Western Australia to Melbourne via places such as Broome, Tanami (Northern Territory), Halls Creek (Western Australia), Alice Springs (Northern Territory), Oodnadatta (South Australia) and Adelaide. Travelling in six-wheeled Morris trucks, his group was accompanied by Eccerty—a cross-breed cattle dog rescued by one of the men, Ernest Officer, before the party left Broome. Eccerty had earned the displeasure of his original owner—and, it seems, half the township—by involving himself in a local football match. Doing what heelers do, he'd taken to the field, snapping at a couple of ankles belonging to members of the opposing team in an effort to bring the unruly group into line. Unfortunately, one of Eccerty's snaps hit its mark and the poor dog suddenly found himself the target of both teams.

When he joined Terry's group, Eccerty was a scared, unhappy and snarling dog. Unused to car travel, his misery was made worse by severe motion sickness during the first few days of the journey. But Eccerty quickly found his motoring legs, got used to life camping in the outback and came to love the men and the travel. In fact, he became so happy in his new role as travel escort that the moment any of the men touched the starting handle—even before the engine fired—Eccerty had leapt into the back of the truck, ready to hit the trail. As the trucks had been stripped of all excess weight, there were no mudguards or running boards— so Eccerty had to do a straight jump of about one metre up to the floorboards, onto the seat then over the back to find his spot among the load. Sometimes this was a precarious perch—one foot in the billy, one on a swag—but Eccerty soon got the hang of life on the road.

Just like his predecessor Girlie, Eccerty was happiest when travelling with his closest human companion, Ernest Officer. If he found himself in the wrong truck, a look of doubt would come over his face before he quickly jumped down and into the right vehicle, letting out a bark of triumph when he was 'home'.

As a cattle dog, Eccerty's weakness was stock work. Any livestock encountered on the way, whether horses, goats, cattle or hens, had to be driven, worked and preferably rounded up: something that did not always meet with the approval of the animals' owner.

Every morning, Eccerty would wake the campers with a series of barks as he ran between each man and was only satisfied when he received a pat. If anyone tried to pull the blankets over their head, Eccerty was up for the challenge, pawing away at the covered head and poking his nose under the blankets until the drowsy man gave up any attempt at further sleep and rewarded him with a pat. Terry called Eccerty 'the life of the camp'.[21]

Always room for one more; a dog squeezes in on one of Terry's later expeditions.

One thing Eccerty didn't appreciate was undue noise. Each evening when one of the men, Ted North, brought out his mouth organ and began to play, Eccerty howled his displeasure, running from swag to swag in the hope that someone would make the dreadful sound stop. The men may not have obliged him then, but he quickly learnt that when the flies got bad, a kindly human would always brush them away from his eyes.

A later expedition would be joined by the aptly named Spot who, like his canine predecessors, was a beloved companion throughout the weeks and months in the outback. Terry's dogs were an important part of his outback adventures, and frequently starred in photographs taken on the trips.

It is clear these outback dogs were loved, both by the expeditioners and the Australian public. For city folk, the inclusion of a dog in a photograph of the Australian desert could soften the image in a way that a picture of dusty, sunburned men could not; it seemed that no matter how harsh the terrain or how hot the sun, the dogs were having a fantastic time. And for the adventurers themselves, isolated in the bush for long stretches, a dog—uncomplaining, brave, defender, loyal friend—meant a person was never truly alone. There was always someone there to confide in, to love and to offer support, laughter and the comfort of physical contact, even when the rest of the world was hundreds of kilometres away.

The End of the Tail

From the moment dingoes arrived on this continent, dogs have played a central role in Australia's history. Incorporated into the life and Dreaming of many Indigenous peoples, the dingo managed to bridge the divide between wild and tame. It claimed a pivotal role in the Australian ecosystem, and the importance of the dingo has not been diminished by the centuries.

In 1788 when the First Fleet dropped anchor in Botany Bay, dogs were with them, eager to disembark. Although Hector the Newfoundland was just one among many dogs on board, the fact that his name was recorded shows just how important he was—not only to John Marshall, his owner, but to other people who had made the long journey from Portsmouth to the new colony. In the same way, all the other First Fleet dogs must have mattered very much to their human companions. These were not just dogs who could make life easier—for example, dogs that could hunt—but dogs who made life more bearable. For the new settlers, so far from home and everything that was familiar, the companionship and love of a dog would have been a special and cherished thing. Early Australian paintings confirm that companion and lapdogs were an important part of colonial society.

More than 200 years later nothing has really changed—in fact, Australians are perhaps closer to their dogs than ever. The National Library holds images of Australian dogs from the late 1800s to today; the pictures in this book represent only a small proportion of the dog photographs in the collections.

A proud and loving dog owner shows off her best friend for the camera, 1936.

Droving cattle in the Victorian High Plains would have been impossible without dogs.

If it wasn't for the style of clothing or the model of a car, in many cases it would be difficult to accurately date some of the photographs. Regardless of whether a picture was taken today or 100 years ago, the connection between people and their dogs shines through. Australians work closely with their dogs, play with them, embrace them, stroke them, comfort and are comforted by them; and, most of all, Australians laugh and smile with their dogs.

As a nation, we embraced a large number of the breeds the dog world has to offer, but we also found that unique Australian conditions occasionally required different canine qualities. This led to the development of iconic dogs such as the kelpie and Australian cattle dog: breeds that have been enthusiastically adopted by farmers around the world. Other Australian breeds may not be as well known, but whether they are working, sporting or companion dogs, they enrich the national culture, as well as the lives of the people who love them.

Based on the wide variety of photographs in the National Library's collections, it seems safe to say that if a part of Australia—however remote—has been visited by a person, there's a good chance that, at some point, someone has taken their dog there too. From the most remote parts of the outback to the subzero climate of the Australian Antarctic Territory, Australia's dogs have been there. Significantly, even if the original reason for taking dogs was a practical one, the people involved quickly discovered the unexpected benefits of canine companionship.

From studio portraits to snapshots, Australians from decades past recorded every aspect of life with dogs. Regardless of whether the dog was the main subject, a casual bystander or the lone canine countenance in a group picture, what mattered was the dog was there. For every Yowie, Bully or Blizzard, there are hundreds more dogs whose names are long forgotten, but whose presence in a photograph tells a story. There are paw prints running through Australia's history.

Artist Paddy Japaljarri Stewart faces his canine critics at the Yuendumu Art Centre, NT, 2003.

Endnotes

Introduction

1. 'What we Collect', National Library of Australia, nla.gov.au/about-us/corporate-documents/policy-and-planning/collection-development-policy/what-we-collect
2. The engraving was reproduced in: George Shaw, *Musei Leveriani Explicatio, Anglica et Latina*, vol.II, London: Impensis Jacobi Parkinson, 1792, opposite p.38.

   Edwards was one of the artists to accompany Joseph Banks on the Endeavour voyage. This image (an engraving taken from his original painting) reconstructs the scene at the Endeavour River, Cape York Peninsula, in 1770. Damage to the ship forced Cook ashore for six weeks but allowed for extended shore observations to be made. This was when Banks first saw a kangaroo; Edwards depicted Banks in the background, using his two greyhounds to hunt (unsuccessfully) the animals.

   In 1800 Edwards went on to produce *Cynographia Britannica*, the first illustrated encyclopedia on the dog breeds of Great Britain.
3. The earliest daguerreotypes required an exposure time of up to 15 minutes, but advances in cameras and the chemical process reduced this to between 60 and 90 seconds and subsequently to under 60 seconds by the early 1840s.
4. F.E.H. Schroeder, 'Say Cheese! The Revolution in the Aesthetics of Smiles', *Journal of Popular Culture*, vol.32, no.2, 1998.
5. Doubtless there were many factors that changed the way people presented themselves for photographs. The move from a serious expression to a smile reflected a general relaxation in social propriety, improved dentistry, and even an increasing desire for popularity that was initially associated with the rise of celebrity culture, but then spread to the general population.
6. Animal Medicines Australia, *Pets in Australia: A National Survey of Pets and People*, Australian Capital Territory: Animal Medicines Australia Pty Ltd, 2019, animalmedicinesaustralia.org.au/wp-content/uploads/2019/10/ANIM001-Pet-Survey-Report19_v1.7_WEB_low-res.pdf

Chapter 1: By Our Sides

1. Juliet Clutton-Brock, *Animals as Domesticates: A World View Through History*, East Lansing: Michigan State University Press, 2012.
2. Several researchers suggest approximately 32,000 years ago, while others believe the evidence points to an even earlier date. See for example: Mietje Germonpré et al., 'Fossil Dogs and Wolves from Palaeolithic Sites in Belgium, the Ukraine and Russia: Osteometry, Ancient DNA and Stable Isotopes', *Journal of Archaeological Science*, vol.36, no.2, 2009, pp.437–490; Greger Larson et al., 'Rethinking Dog Domestication by Integrating Genetics, Archeology, and Biogeography', *Proceedings of the National Academy of Sciences*, vol.109, no.23, 2012, pp.8878–83; Stanley Olsen and John Olsen, 'The Chinese Wolf, Ancestor of New World Dogs', *Science*, vol.197, no.4303, 1977, pp.533–535; Peter Savolainen et al., 'Genetic Evidence for an East Asian Origin of Domestic Dogs', *Science*, vol.298, 2002, pp.1610–13; Pat Shipman, *The Animal Connection: A New Perspective on What Makes Us Human*, New York: W.W. Norton & Company, 2011, p.203; Pontus Skoglund et al., 'Ancient Wolf Genome Reveals an Early Divergence of Domestic Dog Ancestors and Admixture into High-Latitude Breeds', *Current Biology*, vol.25, no.11, 2015, pp.1515–19; Carles Vilà et al., 'Multiple and Ancient Origins of the Domestic Dog', *Science*, vol.276, no.5319, 1997, pp.1687–89; Guo-dong Wang et al., 'The Genomics of

Selection in Dogs and the Parallel Evolution Between Dogs and Humans', *Nature Communications*, vol.4, article no.1860, 2013.

3. Jared Diamond, 'Evolution, Consequences and Future of Plant and Animal Domestication', *Nature*, vol.418, no.6898, 2002, pp.700–707; Hannes Napierala and Hans-Peter Uerpmann, 'A "New" Palaeolithic Dog from Central Europe', *International Journal of Osteoarchaeology*, vol.22, no.2, 2012, pp.127–137.
4. Colin Groves, 'The Advantages and Disadvantages of Being Domesticated', *Perspectives in Human Biology*, vol.4, no.1, 1999, pp.1–12.
5. Based on the short length of the medial digit, the tracks have been identified as those of a dog, not a wolf.
6. Michel Garcia, 'Ichnologie Générale de la Grotte Chauvet', *Bulletin de la Société Préhistorique Française*, vol.102, no.1, 2005, pp.103–108.
7. Support for the 'survival of the friendliest' hypothesis of dog domestication comes from research showing that dogs have differences in their DNA (compared to wolves) that make them more sociable. See for example: Bridgett M. vonHoldt et al., 'Structural Variants in Genes Associated with Human Williams-Beuren Syndrome Underlie Stereotypical Hypersociability in Domestic Dogs', *Science Advances*, vol.3, no.7, 2017.
8. Carlos A. Driscoll et al., 'The Near Eastern Origin of Cat Domestication', *Science*, vol.317, no.5837, 2007, pp.519–523.

   There is however some evidence of a slightly earlier (9,500 years ago) loose association between cats and humans: Yaowu Hu et al., 'Earliest Evidence for Commensal Processes of Cat Domestication', *Proceedings of the National Academy of Sciences*, vol.111, no.1, 2014, pp.116–120; J.-D. Vigne et al., 'Early Taming of the Cat in Cyprus', *Science*, vol.304, no.5668, 2004, p.259.
9. Harriet Ritvo, 'Pride and Pedigree: The Evolution of the Victorian Dog Fancy', *Victorian Studies*, vol.29, no.2, 1986, pp.227–253; Adrian Franklin, *Animals and Modern Cultures: A Sociology of Human-Animal Relations in Modernity*, London: Sage Publishing, 1999, p.14; Keith Thomas, *Man and the Natural World: Changing Attitudes in England 1500–1800*, Hammondsworth: Penguin Books, 1983, p.117.
10. G. Stables, 'Breeding and Rearing for Pleasure, Prizes and Profit', *The Dog Owners' Annual for 1896*, London: Dean and Son, 1896, p.166. As cited in: Harriet Ritvo, *The Animal Estate*, Cambridge, Massachusetts: Harvard University Press, 1989, p.93.
11. 'The Gordon and Irish Setter Cross', *The Australasian* (Melbourne), 25 September 1869, p.395.
12. 'Canine Exhibition', *The Mercury* (Hobart), 13 November 1862, p.2.
13. Statistics for the Colony of Victoria in 1864 indicate that by the end of that year, the population numbered only 605,501 people: Registrar-General's Office, *Statistics of the Colony of Victoria for the Year 1864*, Melbourne: John Ferres, Government Printer, 1866.
14. K. Allen et al., 'Cardiovascular Reactivity and the Presence of Pets, Friends, and Spouses: The Truth About Cats and Dogs', *Psychosomatic Medicine*, vol.64, no.5, 2002, pp.727–739.
15. E. Friedmann and S. Thomas, 'Pet Ownership, Social Support, and One-Year Survival After Acute Myocardial Infarction in the Cardiac Arrhythmia Suppression Trial (CAST)', *The American Journal of Cardiology*, vol.76, no.17, 1995, pp.1213–17; Gregory J. Tranah et al., 'Domestic and Farm-Animal Exposures and Risk of Non-Hodgkin's Lymphoma in a Population-Based Study in the San Francisco Bay Area', *Cancer Epidemiology, Biomarkers & Prevention*, vol.17, no.9, 2008, pp.2382–87; L.A. Hart, 'Positive Effects of Animals for Psychosocially Vulnerable People: a Turning Point for Delivery', in A. Fine (ed.), *Animal-assisted Therapy: Theoretical Foundations and Practical Guidelines* (3rd ed.), Boston:

Elsevier Science and Technology, 2010, pp.59–84; Gregg K. Takashima and Michael J. Day, 'Setting the One Health Agenda and the Human-Companion Animal Bond', *International Journal of Environmental Research and Public Health*, vol.11, no.11, 2014, pp.11110–20; M. Mubanga et al., 'Dog Ownership and the Risk of Cardiovascular Disease and Death – a Nationwide Cohort Study', *Scientific Reports*, vol.7, 2017.

16. D.L. Wells, 'The Effects of Animals on Human Health and Well-being', *Journal of Social Issues*, vol.65, no.3, 2009, pp.523–543.
17. F. Walsh, 'Human-Animal Bonds I: The Relational Significance of Companion Animals', *Family Process*, vol.48, no.4, 2009, pp.462–480.
18. There is no record of a George Henry serving with the 9th Battalion, however several servicemen in this Battalion have George and Henry as their first and middle names, or middle and last names.
19. *Townsville Daily Bulletin*, 16 December 1924, p.4.
20. 'A Clever Dog', *Nowra Leader*, 5 February 1926, p.1.

Chapter 2: The Dingo

1. Bradley Smith et al., 'Taxonomic Status of the Australian Dingo: the Case for Canis Dingo, Meyer, 1793', *Zootaxa*, vol.4564, no.1, 2019, pp.173–197; Kylie M. Cairns, 'What is a Dingo – Origins, Hybridisation and Identity', *Australian Zoologist*, vol.41, no.3, 2021, pp.322–337.
2. See for example: Stephen Jackson et al., 'The Wayward Dog: Is the Australian Native Dog or Dingo a Distinct Species?' *Zootaxa*, vol.4317, no.2, 2017, pp.201–224; Stephen Jackson et al., 'Taxonomy of the Dingo: It's an ancient dog', *Australian Zoologist*, vol.41, no.3, 2021, pp.347–357.
3. Matt A. Field et al., 'The Australian Dingo is an Early Offshoot of Modern Breed Dogs', *Science Advances*, vol.8, no.16, 2022. Bradley Smith et al., 'Taxonomic Status of the Australian Dingo: the Case for Canis Dingo, Meyer, 1793', *Zootaxa*, vol.4564, no.1, 2019, pp.173–197.
4. J.E. Heeres, *The Part Borne by the Dutch in the Discovery of Australia 1606–1765*, London: Royal Dutch Geographical Society, 1899, p.42.
5. While there has been no land bridge between the Asian and Australian continents for several million years, dingoes could have moved down from New Guinea to Australia, which remained connected until about 6,500–8,000 years ago.
6. M.A. Fillios and P.S.C. Taçon, 'Who Let the Dogs in? A Review of the Recent Genetic Evidence for the Introduction of the Dingo to Australia and Implications for the Movement of People', *Journal of Archaeological Science: Reports*, vol.7, 2016, pp.782–792.
7. Some molecular studies suggest the dingo may have arrived in Australia earlier than their occurrence in the fossil record. See for example: K.M. Cairns and A.N. Wilton, 'New Insights on the History of Canids in Oceania Based on Mitochondrial and Nuclear Data', *Genetica*, vol.144, no.5, 2016, pp.553–565; A.H. Freedman et al., 'Genome Sequencing Highlights the Dynamic Early History of Dogs', *PLoS Genetics*, vol.10, no.1, 2014; M.C. Oskarsson et al., 'Mitochondrial DNA Data Indicate an Introduction through Mainland Southeast Asia for Australian Dingoes and Polynesian Domestic Dogs', *Proceedings of the Royal Society B: Biological Sciences*, vol.279, no.1730, 2012, pp.967–974; P. Savolainen et al., 'A Detailed Picture of the Origin of the Australian Dingo, Obtained from the Study of Mitochondrial DNA', *Proceedings of the National Academy of Sciences of the USA*, vol.101, no.33, 2004, pp.12387–90; Loukas Koungoulos and Melanie Fillios, 'Hunting Dogs Down Under? On the Aboriginal Use of Tame Dingoes in Dietary Game Acquisition and its Relevance to Australian Prehistory', *Journal of Anthropological Archaeology*, vol.58, 2020.
8. Dingoes lack copies of the gene AMY2B, which codes for the production of the

pancreatic enzyme amylase, the enzyme responsible for the breakdown of starch within the small intestine. By contrast, domestic dogs have numerous copies of this gene. This means domestic dogs have developed to a point where they can thrive on a starch-rich diet (high in grains) while dingoes are virtually unable to process starch at all. This inability to digest grains is particularly important when considering how closely the dingo is related to domestic dogs. It points to an earlier genetic divergence of the dingo from other canid species, and a lack of contact with agriculture-based human societies.

Compared to domestic dogs, dingoes show distinct differences in single nucleotide polymorphisms (a change in a single DNA building block) and within mitochondrial DNA (DNA within the powerhouse of each cell).

M. Arendt et al., 'Diet Adaptation in Dog Reflects Spread of Prehistoric Agriculture', *Heredity*, vol.117, no.5, 2016, pp.301–306; Arman Ardalan et al., 'Narrow Genetic Basis for the Australian Dingo Confirmed Through Analysis of Paternal Ancestry', *Genetica*, vol.140, no.1, 2012, pp.65–73; Kylie M. Cairns et al., 'Elucidating Biogeographical Patterns in Australian Native Canids Using Genome Wide SNPs', *PLoS One*, vol.13, no.6, 2018, pp.1–25; Kylie M. Cairns and Alan N. Wilton, 'New Insights on the History of Canids in Oceania Based on Mitochondrial and Nuclear Data', *Genetica*, vol.144, no.5, 2016, pp.553–565; Bradley Smith (ed.), *The Dingo Debate: Origins, Behaviour and Conservation*, Clayton South, Victoria: CSIRO Publishing, 2015.

Some of this research has also indicated that three distinct dingo populations exist, further highlighting the necessity for careful dingo conservation and management strategies.

9. See for example: T.M. Newsome et al., 'Resolving the Value of the Dingo in Ecological Restoration', *Restoration Ecology*, vol.23, no.3, 2015, pp.201–208; Angus Emmott, 'The Dingo as a management tool on a beef cattle enterprise in western Queensland', *Australian Zoologist*, vol.41, no.3, 2021, pp.459–466.
10. John Batman, *The Settlement of John Batman in Port Phillip from his Own Journal*, Melbourne: George Slater, 1856, p.11.
11. Samuel Rawson, *Diaries and Papers of Samuel Rawson, 1831–1857*, National Library of Australia, MS 204.
12. M. Letnic et al., 'Does a Top-Predator Provide an Endangered Rodent with Refuge from an Invasive Mesopredator?', *Animal Conservation*, vol.12, no.4, 2009, pp.302–312.
13. M. Letnic et al., 'The Arrival and Impacts of the Dingo', in Alistair Glen and Christopher Dickman (eds), *Carnivores of Australia: Past, Present and Future*, Collingwood, Victoria: CSIRO Publishing, 2014, pp.55–69.
14. Thomas A.A. Prowse et al., 'Ecological and Economic Benefits to Cattle Rangelands of Restoring an Apex Predator', *Journal of Applied Ecology*, vol.52, no.2, 2014, pp.455–466.
15. A.E. Newsome et al., 'The Identity of the Dingo I. Morphological Discriminants of Dingo and Dog Skulls', *Australian Journal of Zoology*, vol.28, no.4, 1980, pp.615–625.
16. Peter Thomson, 'The Behavioural Ecology of Dingoes in North-Western Australia. III Hunting and Feeding Behaviour, and Diet', *Wildlife Research*, vol.19, no.5, 1992, pp.531–541.
17. Smith (ed.), *The Dingo Debate*.
18. Paul Tacon and Colin Pardoe, 'Dogs Make us Human', *Natura Australia*, vol. 27, no. 4, 2002, pp. 52-62.
19. R.G. Gunn, *Bunjils Cave: Aboriginal Rock Art Site (Site 74231/001)*, Melbourne: Ministry for Conservation, 1983; Gunn, 'A Dingo Burial from the Arnhem Land Plateau', *Australian Archaeology*, vol.71, 2010, pp.11–16.
20. J.S. Ryan, 'Plotting an Isogloss—the Location and Types of Aboriginal Names for Native Dog in New South Wales', *Oceania*, vol.35, no.2, 1964, pp.111–123.
21. Fred Cahir and Ian Clark, 'The Historic Importance of the Dingo in Aboriginal

Society in Victoria (Australia): A Reconsideration of the Archival Record', *Anthrozoös*, vol.26, no.2, 2013, pp.185–198.

22. Kate Senior et al., 'Dogs and People in Aboriginal Communities: Exploring the Relationship within the Context of the Social Determinants of Health', *Environmental Health*, vol.6, no.4, 2006, pp.39–46.
23. Deborah Bird Rose, *Dingo Makes Us Human: Life and Land in an Aboriginal Australian Culture*, Cambridge: Cambridge University Press, 1992, p.47.
24. Samantha Phelan, *Conducting Dog Health Programs in Indigenous Communities: A Veterinary Guide*, Larrakia Country, Northern Territory: Animal Management in Rural and Remote Indigenous Communities (AMRRIC), 2007, p.4.

    For a detailed discussion of the dingo's water-finding ability, see: Justine Philip, 'The Waterfinders. A Cultural History of the Australian Dingo', *Australian Zoologist*, vol.41, no.3, 2021, pp.593–607.
25. In this region, favoured dogs were also buried in the same way as humans (bundle burials placed in clefts within a rock shelter).

    K. Mulvaney, 'What to Do on a Rainy Day: Reminiscences of Mirriuwung and Gadjerong Artists', *Rock Art Research*, vol.13, no.1, 1996, pp.3–20.
26. Smith (ed.), *The Dingo Debate*, pp.90–91.
27. Koungoulos and Fillios, 'Hunting Dogs Down Under? On the Aboriginal Use of Tame Dingoes in Dietary Game Acquisition and its Relevance to Australian Prehistory', *Journal of Anthropological Archaeology*.
28. E. Kolig, 'Notes and Comments: Aboriginal Man's Best Foe?', *Mankind*, vol.9, no.2, 1973, pp.122–123; Kate Senior et al., 'Dogs and People in Aboriginal Communities: Exploring the Relationship within the Context of the Social Determinants of Health'.
29. Senior et al., 'Dogs and People in Aboriginal Communities: Exploring the Relationship within the Context of the Social Determinants of Health'.

    The authors use the term 'Jankantjara people' when referring to the Yankunytjatjara people.
30. Smith (ed.), *The Dingo Debate*, p.94.
31. Thanks to Wiradjuri descendant Michelle Griffiths for providing considerable insight into the importance of the dingo in Aboriginal culture.
32. Oliver Costello et al., 'A Statement on the Cultural Importance of the Dingo', *Australian Zoologist*, vol.41, no. 3, 2021, pp.296–297.
33. Rose, *Dingo Makes Us Human*.
34. R. Gunn et al., 'A Dingo Burial from the Arnhem Land Plateau'; C. Pardoe, 'Dogs Changed the World', *National Dingo News*, spring 1996, pp.19–29.
35. B. Smith et al., 'Co-existing with Dingoes: Challenges and Solutions to Implementing Non-lethal Management', *Australian Zoologist*, vol.41, no.3, 2020, pp.491–510.
36. See for example: C.R. Dickman et al., 'Reintroducing the Dingo: Can Australia's Conservation Wastelands be Restored?', in M.W. Hayward and M.J. Somers (eds), *Reintroduction of Top-order Predators*, Oxford: John Wiley & Sons, 2009, pp.238–269; Tim S. Doherty et al., 'Continental Patterns in the Diet of a Top Predator: Australia's Dingo', *Mammal Review*, vol.49, no.1, 2018; Justine Philip, 'The Dingo Barrier Fence: Presenting the Case to Decommission the World's Longest Environmental Barrier in the United Nations Decade on Ecosystem Restoration 2021–2030', *Biologia Futura*, vol.73, no.1, 2022, pp.9-27.
37. See for example: A.E. Newsome et al., 'Two Ecological Universes Separated by the Dingo Barrier Fence in Semi-Arid Australia: Interactions Between Landscapes, Herbivory and Carnivory, With and Without Dingoes', *The Rangeland Journal*, vol.23, no.1, 2001, pp.71–98; A.R. Pople et al., 'Trends in the Numbers of Red Kangaroos and Emus on Either Side of the South Australian Dingo Fence: Evidence for Predator Regulation?' *Wildlife Research*, vol.27, no.3, 2000,

pp.269–276; Keith Bradby et al., 'Ecological Connectivity or Barrier Fence? Critical Choices on the Agricultural Margins of Western Australia', *Ecological Management & Restoration*, vol.15, no.3, 2014, pp.180–190; M. Lurgi et al., 'Eradicating Abundant Invasive Prey Could Cause Unexpected and Varied Biodiversity Outcomes: The Importance of Multispecies Interactions', *Journal of Applied Ecology*, vol.55, no.5, 2018, pp.2396–2407.

38. See for example: Chris N. Johnson and Arian D. Wallach, 'The Virtuous Circle: Predator-Friendly Farming and Ecological Restoration in Australia', *Restoration Ecology*, vol.24, no.6, 2016, pp.821–826.
39. See for example: Lee R. Allen, 'Wild Dog Control Impacts on Calf Wastage in Extensive Beef Cattle Enterprises', *Animal Production Science*, vol.54, no.2, 2014, pp.214–220; Arian D. Wallach et al., 'More than Mere Numbers: The Impact of Lethal Control on the Social Stability of a Top-Order Predator', *PLoS One*, vol.4, no.9, 2009, pp.1–8.
40. Costello et al., 'A Statement on the Cultural Importance of the Dingo'.
41. Roland Breckwoldt, *A Very Elegant Animal: The Dingo*, Sydney: Angus and Robertson, 1988, p.264.

Chapter 3: On the Farm

1. F.M. Bladen, Alexander Britton and James Cook (eds), *Historical Records of New South Wales*, Sydney: Government Printer, 1892, vol.V, p.137.
2. Sydenham Teast Edwards, *Cynographia Britannica*, London: C. Whittingham, 1800 [-1805] np.
3. 'High Class Sheep Dogs', *The Carcoar Chronicle* (New South Wales), 24 July 1903, p.4; 'The Kennel', *The Sydney Mail and New South Wales Advertiser*, 20 July 1904, p.135; 'Dog Trials at the Sheepbreeders' Show', *The Sydney Mail and New South Wales Advertiser*, 5 July 1902, p.6.
4. 'Sheep Dog Trials', The Sydney Stock and Station Journal, 23 May 1902, p.9; 'The Kennel', *The Sydney Mail and New South Wales Advertiser*, 8 July 1903, p.69.
5. See for example: *The Australasian* (Melbourne), 10 December 1904, p.13.
6. 'Sheep Dog Trials', *The Horsham Times*, 30 May 1902, p.1.
7. 'The Collie Hindhope Jed', *The Australasian* (Melbourne), 8 August 1903, p.315.
8. Tony Parsons, *The Kelpie: The Definitive Guide to the Australian Working Dog*, Camberwell, Victoria: Viking, 2010.
9. Robert Kaleski, *Australian Barkers and Biters* (2nd ed.), Sydney: The Endeavour Press, 1933, p.93.
10. See for example: 'Barkers and Biters: Robert Kaleski's Great Book', *The Sydney Stock and Station Journal*, 24 April 1914, p.9; 'Origin of the Kelpie', *Warialda Standard and Northern Districts' Advertiser* (New South Wales), 20 February 1950, p.3.

    And examples of those questioning Kaleski's account: 'The Kelpie. His Origin Discussed – Fallacies Exposed', *Sunday Times* (Perth), 16 April 1911, p.12; 'Origins of Kelpie Dogs', *Western Mail* (Perth), 10 March 1927, p.8; 'Breed of the Kelpie', *Daily Advertiser* (Wagga Wagga), 19 January 1948, p.2.
11. T. Chew et al., 'Genomic Characteristics of External Morphology Traits in Kelpies Does Not Support Common Ancestry with the Australian Dingo', *Genes*, vol.10, no.5, 2019, p.337.
12. *Victoria: Crown land licenses*, Melbourne: John Ferres, Government Printer, 1856, vol. II, p.8.
13. There are many theories about the meaning behind the name 'Kelpie' and this seems the most likely. For an account of some other possibilities, see: Parsons, *The Kelpie: The Definitive Guide to the Australian Working Dog*.
14. Wyalong, 'The Origin of the Kelpie', *The Australasian* (Melbourne), 7 May 1921, p.4.

15. 'Pastoral and Agricultural Show at Burrangong', *Australian Town and Country Journal* (Sydney), 29 April 1871, p.6.
16. 'Forbes Pastoral and Agricultural Show', *The Sydney Mail and New South Wales Advertiser*, 9 August 1879, p.217.
17. 'Forbes Pastoral and Agricultural Exhibition', *The Burrangong Argus* (New South Wales), 13 August 1879, pp.2–3.

    In sheepdog trials, 'hurdles' refers to lightweight frames that join together to make a portable enclosure.
18. 'Kennel', *The Queenslander* (Brisbane), 26 April 1902, p.903.
19. See for example: *The Land* (Sydney), 18 May 1951, p.39.
20. 'Highland Sheepdogs for South Australia', *The Register* (Adelaide), 6 September 1910, p.5.
21. 'Kennel Gossip by Wattlebark', *The Australasian* (Melbourne), 9 February 1901, p.14.
22. Noreen R. Clark, *A Dog Called Blue: The Australian Cattle Dog and Stumpy Tail Cattle Dog 1840–2000*. Wallacia, New South Wales: WriteLight Pty Ltd for Noreen R Clark, 2003, p.9.
23. It has been suggested that shortly after Thomas Hall's death, a man named Jack Timmins acquired one or more of the stumpy tailed Hall's heelers and developed them as a specific line, known as Timmin's biters.
24. R. Kaleski, 'Cattle Dogs', *The Agricultural Gazette of New South Wales*, vol.14, August 1903, pp.752–758.
25. 'Cattle Dog Standard', *Australian Town and Country Journal* (Sydney), 19 September 1906, p.9. See also: Australian Cattle Dog Club of NSW Inc and Australian National Kennel Council, *Extended Breed Standard of the Australian Cattle Dog*, New South Wales: Australian National Kennel Council, 2009, p.4, ankc.org.au/media/pdf/635576344152806822_674410ad-df4c-424f-ab70-d0fbf26dadb3.pdf; 'Cattle Dogs', *The Sydney Stock and Station Journal*, 14 August 1903, p.9.
26. Clark, *A Dog Called Blue*, p.56.
27. Australian Cattle Dog Club of NSW Inc and Australian National Kennel Council, *Extended Breed Standard of the Australian Cattle Dog*, 2009, p.5.
28. Walter Beilby, *The Dog in Australasia*, Melbourne: George Robertson and Co, 1897, p.306.
29. 'Stumpy-Tailed Cattle Dogs', *The Australasian* (Melbourne), 14 October 1882, p.24.
30. 'Stumpy-Tailed Cattle Dogs', *The Australasian* (Melbourne), 11 November 1882, p.11.
31. M. von Stephanitz [translated by J. Schwabacher], *The German Shepherd Dog in Word and Picture*, Jena, Germany: Anton Kampfe, 1923.
32. F. Freeman Lloyd, 'Dogs in Australasia III', *The Field*, no.2509, 26 January 1901, p.135.
33. 'Koolie Fundamentals', Koolie Club of Australia, koolie.net/koolie-fundamentals

Chapter 4: Other Australians

1. Peter Cunningham, *Two Years in New South Wales*, vol.1, London: Henry Colburn, 1827, p.314.
2. 'The Australian Rough Terrier Club,' *Leader* (Melbourne), 13 April 1889, p.21.
3. Beilby, *The Dog in Australasia*, p.395.
4. F. Freedman Lloyd, 'Dogs in Australasia IV', *The Field*, no.2510, 2 February 1901, p.155.
5. Australian National Kennel Council, *Extended Breed Standard of the Australian Terrier*, 2011, ankc.org.au/media/pdf/635576247074834368_337ce152-505b-43f2-82e8-721ea43eab10.pdf
6. For example: *The Daily Telegraph* (Sydney), 11 June 1904, p.17; *The Sydney Morning Herald*, 7 September 1904, p.4.
7. 'Murray River Retriever Breed Standard', Australian National Kennel Council, 2021,

ankc.org.au/Breed/Detail/233; *Murray River Retriever Genetic Study*, Wisdom Health, Second edition 2018.

8. Thanks to Karen Bell and the Murray River Retriever Association Inc for information on this breed.

Chapter 5: Australia's Antarctic Huskies

1. Dionise Settle, *The Second Voyage of Master Martin Frobisher, Made to the West and North-West Regions in the year 1577, with a Description of the Country and People*, as quoted in: Richard Hakluyt, *Voyages in Search of the North-West Passage*, London: Cassell & Company, 1886, pp.109–110.
2. *The Herald* (Melbourne), 19 November 1949, p.13.
3. A group of dogs remained in Melbourne, and while the Zoo hoped to keep a breeding pair of each of both the Labrador and Greenland types of husky, there was some uncertainty regarding what to do with the rest. There had been a plan to send dogs to the Snowy Hydro-electric Scheme, presumably to be used for hauling construction material, but this was vetoed by quarantine officials. According to Zoo records (minutes of a meeting of the full board, Melbourne Zoological Gardens, 25 August 1950), the Australian National Antarctic Research Expeditions (ANARE) ultimately decided to take all the 'surplus' huskies.
4. According to *The Herald*, the dogs were equipped with specially made boots, which they would wear until their paws became accustomed to snow and ice. Each dog would initially be fed two pounds of meat once a day, then provisioned entirely on seal meat once they had settled on Heard Island. *The Herald* (Melbourne), 23 January 1950, p.3.
5. Wilkes was established in 1957, one of a number of American stations set up to carry out research in Antarctica during the International Geophysical Year (IGY) which involved 67 countries in numerous scientific research projects. Its timing marked the end of a long period in the Cold War, during which scientific collaboration between nations was severely curtailed. In 1959, the Americans scaled back their activity at Wilkes, and Australia took over operational command of the base. Two years later, Wilkes Station came under the exclusive control of the ANARE.
6. Patrick Moonie, 'Memories of Dog Sledging at Mawson', *Aurora*, vol.8, no.1, 1988, pp.38–45.
7. Rod Ledingham, *The ANARE Antarctic Dog Driver's Manual*, Australia: Xlibris, 2016.
8. NAA, *P1556, Report on Dogs - Mawson 1954.*
9. NAA, *P1556, Dogs and Sledging Report - Davis 1962.*
10. NAA, *P1556, Report on Dogs - Mawson 1954.*
11. W. Pyper, 'Antarctic Place Names Go to the Dogs', *Australian Antarctic Magazine*, no.33, December 2017, p.24.

    Roald Amundsen gave Lassesen to Douglas Mawson. This husky took his name from the original Lassesen, a dog in Amundsen's 1911 South Pole expedition.

Chapter 6: Mascots

1. E.S. Forster, 'Dogs in Ancient Warfare', *Greece and Rome*, vol.10, no.30, 1941, pp.114–117; Helen Johnson, 'The Portrayal of the Dog on Greek Vases', *The Classical Weekly*, vol.12, no.27, 1919, pp.209–213; B.K.B. Fitzgerald, 'Human-Animal Relationships in Ancient Rome.' MA thesis, University of Nebraska, Omaha, 2009.

   An example of war dogs in ancient Egyptian art can be found on the Victory Stele of Ramesses II (1279–1213 BC). This celebrates his triumph over the Hittites at the Battle of Kadesh and includes a number of dogs, including a greyhound-type and a mastiff-type.
2. Kenneth F. Kitchell Jr, 'Man's Best Friend? The Changing Role of the Dog in Greek Society' [conference presentation], *Man and Animals in Antiquity: Proceedings of the Conference at the Swedish Institute in Rome*, Rome, 2004.

3. Eva Scott, Rupert Prince Palatine, Westminster, UK: A. Constable & Co., 1899; Eliot G. Warburton, *Memoirs of Prince Rupert and the Cavaliers including their private correspondence*. London: Richard Bentley, 1849.
4. The painting is attributed to Giuseppe Chiesa.
5. 'Regimental Pets', *Mudgee Guardian and North-Western Representative*, 22 June 1900, p.5.

   Mascots including wallabies, a ringtail possum, a terrier and a 'full-blooded dingo' are also recorded as accompanying the troops to South Africa. See: *The Sydney Morning Herald*, 26 June 1900, p.5; Robert Wallace, *The Australians at the Boer War*, Canberra: Australian War Memorial, 1976, p.236; Don Pedlar, 'Dogs and Other Mascots', *Sabretache*, vol.36, no.1, 1995, pp.30–33.
6. *Sydney Mail*, 3 March 1900, p.515.

   The report of Bushie's death also emphasised the 'mutual affection that exists between a bushman and his dog': *The Sydney Morning Herald*, 19 October 1906, p.5.
7. Frederick Darley was elected Lieutenant Governor in 1891. The name Bushie was also the name applied to the soldiers themselves as members of the Australian Bushmen's Contingent.
8. Bushie died in 1906 at the Red House in Salisbury, where he was under the charge of the King's Land Steward. *The Sydney Morning Herald*, 19 October 1906, p.5.

   See also: Pedlar, 'Dogs and other mascots', pp.30–33.
9. *The Argus* (Melbourne), 8 June 1901, p.14.
10. Winifred Ethelwyn Kelly, *Nelson*, 1901, oil on canvas, 51 x 76.4 cm, collection Australian War Memorial, accession number ART92197.
11. Bugler was initially used to raise funds to equip the South Australian Bushmen's Corps via successive auctions. Originally purchased by the politician J.C.F. Johnson, Bugler was put up for auction. The only two rules of sale were: that in being knocked down, the horse was immediately put up for sale again; non-delivery was to be expected. In this way, over £2,500 was raised with more than £10,000 subsequently brought in through copycat fundraising auctions. See for example: *The Bunyip* (Gawler, South Australia), 9 February 1900, p.2; *The Advertiser* (Adelaide), 28 May 1904, p.10 and 20 June 1904, p.5.
12. See for example: *The Advertiser* (Adelaide), 22 July 1901, p.5.
13. *The Advertiser* (Adelaide), 8 November 1901, p.4.
14. *The Northern Argus* (Clare, South Australia), 25 October 1901, p.2. The 1911 census records a total population of 624 people for Auburn. That a town of this size could raise what equates to approximately £700 (over AU$1,100) in today's money is evidence of both patriotism and the impact of animals on humans.
15. The memorial was the work of Adrian Jones (1845–1938). It is located at the corner of North Terrace and King William Street, Adelaide.
16. Peter Cochrane, *Simpson and the Donkey: The Making of a Legend*, Melbourne: Melbourne University Press, 1992, pp.139–141.
17. 'A Battalion Mascot Lost', *The Brisbane Courier*, 13 April 1916, p.7; 'Yorketown's 10th Batt. Mascot', *The Pioneer* (South Australia), 13 October 1917, p.2; 'A Company Mascot', *The Bendigo Independent*, 9 September 1915, p.6; 'Mascot Proves Fickle', *The Herald* (Melbourne), 19 May 1919, p.2; 'Lithgow Boys' Mascot', *Lithgow Mercury*, 4 September 1914, p.4; 'The British Bulldog', *Warrnambool Standard*, 19 November 1914, p.4; 'Of the Bulldog Breed', *The Mirror* (Sydney), 25 May 1919, p.1; 'Savage Bulldog is Tamed and is Now Mascot of Unit', *The Herald* (Melbourne), 21 July 1917, p.5.
18. *The Australasian* (Melbourne), September 12 1914, p.56.
19. 'The Bulldog Breed at Flinders Naval Depot', *The Advocate* (Burnie, Tasmania), 29 December 1939, p.7; '5-Month-Old Puppy Now Real Digger', *News* (Adelaide),

13 October 1939, p.5; 'Roger the Lodger Puckapunyal's Favorite', *The Herald* (Melbourne), 28 December 1939, p.2; 'Navy's Bulldog Mascot, Bill, Gets His X-Ray', *The Herald* (Melbourne), 5 January 1943, p.3; 'Bulldog Leads Navy March', *The Courier-Mail* (Brisbane), 24 July 1941, p.5; 'Navy Mascot "Killed In Action"', *The Daily News* (Perth), 1 April 1947, p.10.

20. Sergeant Wilson (service number 26) was awarded the Meritorious Service Medal, gazetted on 28 December 1917. He was discharged at the end of the war and returned to Australia in 1919. Australian Military Forces, 'Wilson James Reginald', NAA:B2455, WILSON J R 26.
21. 'Tasmania's Fortieth', *Daily Telegraph* (Launceston), 15 May 1916, p.6.
22. See for example: K. Allen et al., 'Pet Ownership, but Not ACE inhibitor Therapy, Blunts Home Blood Pressure Responses to Mental Stress', *Hypertension*, vol.38, no.4, 2001, pp.815–820; John Polheber and Robert Matchock, 'The Presence of a Dog Attenuates Cortisol and Heart Rate in the Trier Social Stress Test Compared to Human Friends', *Journal of Behavioral Medicine*, vol.37, no.5, 2014, pp.860–867; Karen M. Allen et al., 'Presence of Human Friends and Pet Dogs as Moderators of Autonomic Responses to Stress in Women', *Journal of Personality and Social Psychology*, vol.61, no.4, 1991, pp.582–589; E. Friedmann et al., 'Social Interaction and Blood Pressure. Influence of Animal Companions', *The Journal of Nervous and Mental Disease*, vol.171, no.8, 1983, pp.461–465.
23. See for example: Brian T. Gregg, 'Crossing the Berm: An Occupational Therapist's Perspective on Animal-Assisted Therapy in a Deployed Environment', *U.S. Army Medical Department Journal*, April–June 2012, pp.55–56; L. Fike et al., 'Occupational Therapists as Dog Handlers: the Collective Experience with Animal-Assisted Therapy in Iraq', *U.S. Army Medical Department Journal*, April–June 2012, pp.51–54; William Krol, 'Training the Combat and Operational Stress Control Dog: an Innovative Modality for Behavioral Health', *U.S. Army Medical Department Journal*, April–June 2012, pp.46–50.

    During the Iraq War (2003–2011) specially trained stress-relief dogs were regularly sent to Iraq to assist United States soldiers on combat deployment.

    See: Adam Ashton, 'These Dogs of War Offer 4-legged Therapy', *The News Tribune* (Tacoma, United States), 12 February, 2011, p.1.
24. As cited in: J. Cooper, *Animals in War*, London: Corgi Books, 1984, p.105.

Chapter 7: Outback Dogs

1. Gregory Mathews, *The Birds of Australia*, London: Witherby, 1910–1927.
2. 'Overlanding by Cycle, Fremantle to Sydney', *Kalgoorlie Western Argus*, 25 December 1906, p.30.
3. 'Dorgs', *The Sun* (Sydney), 18 June 1939, p.3.
4. Malcolm Ellis, *The Long Lead: Across Australia by Motor-car*, London: T Fisher Unwin, 1927, p.94.
5. 'Birtles' Car', *The Sunday Times* (Perth), 17 June 1928, p.6.
6. Francis Birtles, *Battle Fronts of Outback*, Sydney: Angus & Robertson, 1935.
7. Birtles, *Battle Fronts of Outback*, p.43.
8. Birtles, *Battle Fronts of Outback*, p.45.
9. 'Picture Hunt', *The Sun* (Sydney), 16 August 1914, p.10. While the journalist mentions alligators, presumably he means freshwater crocodiles.
10. 'Across Australia — in the track of Burke and Wills', *The Mirror of Australia* (Sydney), 5 February 1916, p.6.
11. Birtles, *Battle Fronts of Outback*, p.68.
12. 'Through Northern Wilds', *The Sun* (Sydney), 27 July 1914, p.7.
13. 'Birtles' Pal', *Truth* (Brisbane), 28 May 1922, p.1; 'Dinkum. Birtles' Wonder Dog', *The Daily Telegraph* (Sydney), 28 May 1924, p.8; 'Dinkum. The story of a dog', *The Bunbury Herald and Blackwood Express*, 7 October

1927, p.2.

14. Birtles' second Bean car is part of the National Museum of Australia collection.
15. Ellis, *The Long Lead*, p.212.
16. Ellis, *The Long Lead*, p.148.
17. 'Post-Flood Conditions. Experiences of Birtles', *The Advertiser* (Adelaide), 20 May 1930, p.17; 'Dog Explorer at Alsatian Show', *The Register News-Pictorial* (Adelaide), 8 December 1930, p.22.
18. 'Parade of Alsatians', *The Mail* (Adelaide), 6 December 1930, p.8.
19. Some accounts have this trip departing from Longreach, Queensland. Michael Terry, *Across Unknown Australia*, London: Herbert Jenkins Ltd, 1925.
20. The British-made Guy Roadless Vehicles were essentially trucks fitted with caterpillar tracks instead of rear wheels; great for traction but prone to serious wear on the track joints and always in danger of overheating if pushed too hard.

    The journey was filmed by Pathé Frère and screened to an invitation-only audience under the title *The Grip of Wanderlust*. The film has since been lost.
21. Michael Terry, *Hidden Wealth and Hiding People*, Putnam, London, 1931, p.138.

Bibliography

Allen, K., et al., 'Pet Ownership, but Not ACE inhibitor Therapy, Blunts Home Blood Pressure Responses to Mental Stress', *Hypertension*, vol. 38, no. 4, 2001, pp. 815–820.

—, 'Presence of Human Friends and Pet Dogs as Moderators of Autonomic Responses to Stress in Women', *Journal of Personality and Social Psychology*, vol. 61, no. 4, 1991, pp. 582–589.

—, 'Cardiovascular Reactivity and the Presence of Pets, Friends, and Spouses: The Truth About Cats and Dogs', *Psychosomatic Medicine*, vol. 64, no. 5, 2002, pp. 727–739.

Allen, Lee R., 'Wild Dog Control Impacts on Calf Wastage in Extensive Beef Cattle Enterprises', *Animal Production Science*, vol. 54, no. 2, 2014, pp. 214–220.

Allsopp, Nigel, *Australian War Dogs*. Chatswood, NSW: New Holland, 2012.

—, *Animals in Combat*. London: New Holland, 2014.

Amundsen, Roald, *The South Pole: an account of the Norwegian Antarctic Expedition in the "Fram", 1910-12*, vol. I, Translated by A. G. Chater, London: John Murray, 1912.

Animal Medicines Australia, *Pets in Australia: A national survey of pets and people*, ACT: Animal Medicines Australia Pty Ltd, 2019.

Arendt, M., Cairns, K.M., et al., 'Diet Adaptation in Dog Reflects Spread of Prehistoric Agriculture', *Heredity*, vol. 117, no. 5, 2016, pp. 301-306.

Ardalan, A., Oskarsson, M., et al., 'Narrow Genetic Basis for the Australian Dingo Confirmed Through Analysis of Paternal Ancestry', *Genetica*, vol. 140, no. 1, 2012, pp. 65-73.

Australian Cattle Dog Club of NSW Inc and Australian National Kennel Council, *Extended Breed Standard of the Australian Cattle Dog*, New South Wales: Australian National Kennel Council, 2009.

Australian National Kennel Council, Extended Breed Standard of the Australian Terrier, New South Wales: Australian National Kennel Council, 2011, ankc.org.au/media/pdf/635576247074834368_337ce152-505b-43f2-82e8-721ea43eab10.pdf

Australian National Kennel Council, Murray River Retriever breed standard, New South Wales: Australian National Kennel Council, 2021, https://ankc.org.au/Breed/Detail/233

Balme, J., O'Connor, S. and Fallon, S., 'New dates

on dingo bones from Madura Cave provide oldest firm evidence for arrival of the species in Australia', *Scientific Reports*, vol. 8, no. 9933, 2018. doi.org/10.1038/s41598-018-28324-x.

Batman, John, *The Settlement of John Batman in Port Phillip from his Own Journal*. Melbourne: George Slater, 1856.

Beilby, Walter, *The Dog in Australasia*. Melbourne: George Robertson and Co., 1897.

Bertrand, Ina, 'Francis Birtles - Cyclist, Explorer, Kodaker', *Cinema Papers*, January 1974, pp. 30-35.

Birtles, Francis, *Battle Fronts of Outback*. Sydney: Angus & Robertson, 1935.

Bladen, F.M. et al. (eds), *Historical records of New South Wales*. Sydney: Government Printer, 1892.

Bowlby, John, *Attachment and Loss (vol. 1. Attachment)*, New York: Basic Books, 1969.

Bradby, Keith, et al., 'Ecological Connectivity or Barrier Fence? Critical Choices on the Agricultural Margins of Western Australia', *Ecological Management & Restoration*, vol. 15, no. 3, 2014, pp. 180–190.

Brawata, R.L., 'Does management of a top carnivore influence the response of mesopredators and prey to rainfall in arid ecosystems? Evidence for a Baseline Density theory', *Australian Zoologist*, vol. 41, no. 3, 2021, pp. 417–432. doi.org/10.7882/AZ.2021.007.

Breckwoldt, Roland, *A Very Elegant Animal: The Dingo*. Sydney: Angus and Robertson, 1988.

Brown, Warren, *Francis Birtles*. Sydney: Hachette, 2012.

Cahir, F., and Clark, I., 'The Historic Importance of the Dingo in Aboriginal Society in Victoria (Australia): A Reconsideration of the Archival Record', *Anthrozoös*, vol. 26, no. 2, 2013, pp. 185-198.

Cairns, K.M. 'What is a dingo – origins, hybridisation and identity', *Australian Zoologist*, vol. 41, no. 3, 2021, pp. 322–337. doi.org/10.7882/AZ.2021.004.

Cairns, K.M., Crowther, M., et al. 'The myth of wild dogs in Australia: are there any out there?' *Australian Mammalogy*, vol. 44, 2022, pp. 67-75. doi.org/10.1071/AM20055.

Cairns, K.M., Shannon, L.M. et al., 'Elucidating Biogeographical Patterns in Australian Native Canids Using Genome Wide SNPs', *PLoS One*, vol. 13, no. 6, 2018, pp. 1-25.

Cairns, K.M., and Wilton, A.N., 'New insights on the history of canids in Oceania based on mitochondrial and nuclear data', *Genetica*, vol. 144, no. 5, 2016, pp. 553–565. doi.org/10.1007/s10709-016-9924-z.

Chester, Jonathan, *Huskies. Polar Sledge Dogs*. Sydney: Margaret Hamilton Books, 1994.

Chew, T., et al., 'Genomic Characteristics of External Morphology Traits in Kelpies Does Not Support Common Ancestry with the Australian Dingo', *Genes*, vol. 10, no. 5, 2019, p. 337.

Clark, Noreen R., *A Dog Called Blue. The Australian Cattle Dog and Stumpy Tail Cattle Dog 1840-2000*. WriteLight Pty Ltd for Noreen R Clark: Wallacia, NSW, 2003.

Clutton-Brock, Juliet, A*nimals as Domesticates: A World View Through History*, East Lansing: Michigan State University Press, 2012.

Cochrane, Peter, *Simpson and the Donkey*. Melbourne: Melbourne University Press, 1992.

Cooper, J., *Animals in War*. London: Corgi Books, 1984.

Corbett, L. and Newsome, A.F., 'Dingo Society and its Maintenance: a Preliminary Analysis', in M. Fox (ed.), *The Wild Canids: Their Systematics, Behavioural Ecology and Evolution*. New York: Van Nostrand Reinhold, 1975.

Costello, O., Webster, N., Morgan, D., 'A statement on the cultural importance of the dingo', *Australian Zoologist*, vol. 41 no. 3, 2021, pp. 296–297. doi.org/10.7882/AZ.2021.028.

Cunningham, *Peter, Two Years in New South Wales: comprising sketches of the actual state of society in that colony, of its peculiar advantages to emigrants, of its topography, natural history, &c. &c*. vol. 1. London: Henry Colburn, 1827.

Curtis, Paul, *A History of Professional Photography in Australia*. Mona Vale, NSW: Rose Publishing Co., 2013.

Dennis, Peter (ed.), *The Oxford Companion to*

Australian Military History. South Melbourne, Vic: Oxford University Press, 2008.

Dewar, Mickey, 'Michael Terry: The Last Explorer?' *Journal of Northern Territory History*, no. 20, 2009, pp. 51-74.

Diamond, Jared, 'Evolution, Consequences, and Future of Plant and Animal Domestication', *Nature*, vol. 418, no. 6898, 2002, pp.700-707.

Dickman, C.R., Glen A., et al., 'Reintroducing the Dingo: Can Australia's Conservation Wastelands be Restored?' in M.W. Hayward & M.J. Somers (eds), *Reintroduction of Top-order Predators*. Oxford, UK: John Wiley & Sons, 2009, pp. 238-269.

Doherty, Tim S., et al., 'Continental Patterns in the Diet of a Top Predator: Australia's Dingo', *Mammal Review*, vol.49, no.1, 2018.

Driscoll, C.A., Menotti-Raymond, M., et al., 'The Near Eastern Origin of Cat Domestication', *Science*, vol. 317, no. 5837, 2007, pp. 519-523.

Edwards, Sydenham T., *Cynographia Britannica*. London: C. Whittingham, 1800 [-1805].

Elledge, A.E., Leung, L.K., et al., 'Assessing the Taxonomic Status of Dingoes *Canis familiaris dingo* for Conservation', *Mammal Review*, vol. 36, no. 2, 2006, pp. 142-156.

Ellis, M.H., *The Long Lead: Across Australia by Motor Car*. London: T Fisher Unwin, 1927.

Emmott, Angus. 'The Dingo as a management tool on a beef cattle enterprise in western Queensland', *Australian Zoologist*, vol. 41, no. 3, 2021, pp. 459-466.

Ennis, Helen, *Intersections*. Canberra: National Library of Australia, 2004.

Field, M.A., Yadav, S., et al. 'The Australian dingo is an early offshoot of modern breed dogs', *Science Advances*, vol. 8, no. 16, 2022. doi.org/10.1126/sciadv.abm5944.

Fike, L., Najera, C., et al., 'Occupational Therapists as Dog Handlers: the Collective Experience with Animal-Assisted Therapy in Iraq', *U.S. Army Medical Department Journal*, April-June, 2012, pp. 51-54.

Fillios, M.A. and Taçon, P. S.C., 'Who let the dogs in? A review of the recent genetic evidence for the introduction of the dingo to Australia and implications for the movement of people', *Journal of Archaeological Science*: Reports, vol. 7, 2016, pp. 782-792. doi.org/10.1016/j.jasrep.2016.03.001.

Fitzgerald, B.K.B., 'Human-Animal Relationships in Ancient Rome.' MA thesis, University of Nebraska, Omaha, 2009.

Forster, E.S., 'Dogs in Ancient Warfare', *Greece and Rome*, vol. 10, no. 30, 1941, pp. 114-117.

Franklin, Adrian, *Animals and Modern Cultures*. London: Sage Publications, 1999.

Frantz, L.A.F., Mullin, V., et al., 'Genomic and Archaeological Evidence Suggest a Dual Origin of Domestic Dogs', *Science*, vol. 352, no. 6290, 2016, pp. 1228-1231.

Freedman, A.H., Gronau, I. et al., 'Genome Sequencing Highlights the Dynamic Early History of Dogs' *PLoS Genet*, vol. 10, no. 1, 2014, e1004016, doi.org/10.1371/journal.pgen.1004016.

Freeman Lloyd, F., 'Dogs in Australasia III', *The Field*, no. 2509, 26 January 1901, p. 135.

— 'Dogs in Australasia IV', *The Field*, no. 2510, 2 February 1901, p. 155.

Friedmann, E., Katcher, A.H., et al., 'Social Interaction and Blood Pressure. Influence of Animal Companions', *The Journal Of Nervous And Mental Disease*, vol. 171, no. 8, 1983, pp. 461-465.

Friedmann, E., and Krause-Parello, C.A., 'Companion animals and human health: benefits, challenges, and the road ahead for human—animal interaction', *Revue scientifique et technique*, vol. 37, no. 1, 2018, pp. 71-75.

Friedmann, E., and Thomas, S., 'Pet Ownership, Social Support, and One-Year Survival After Acute Myocardial Infarction in the Cardiac Arrhythmia Suppression Trial (CAST)', *The American Journal of Cardiology*, vol. 76, no. 17, 1995, pp. 1213-1217.

Fry, Roy, *Back o'beyond with two men and a dog: outback adventure in retrospect*, unpublished manuscript, National Library of Australia, MS 953.

Garcia, Michel, 'Ichnologie Générale de la Grotte Chauvet', *Bulletin de la Société Préhistorique*

Française, vol. 102, no. 1, 2005, pp. 103-108.

Germonpré, M., Sablin, M.V., et al., 'Fossil Dogs and Wolves From Palaeolithic Sites in Belgium, the Ukraine and Russia: Osteometry, Ancient DNA and Stable Isotopes', *Journal of Archaeological Science*, vol. 36, no. 2, 2009, pp. 437-490.

Gregg, Brian T. 'Crossing the Berm: an Occupational Therapist's Perspective on Animal-Assisted Therapy in a Deployed Environment', *U.S. Army Medical Department Journal*, April-June, 2012, pp. 55-56.

Groves, Colin, 'The Advantages and Disadvantages of Being Domesticated', *Perspectives in Human Biology*, vol. 4, no. 1, 1999, pp. 1-12.

Gunn, R., Whear, R.L., et al., 'A Dingo Burial From the Arnhem Land Plateau', *Australian Archaeology*, vol. 71, 2010, pp. 11-16.

Gunn, R.G., *Bunjils Cave: aboriginal rock art site (Site 74231/001)*. Melbourne: Victoria Archaeological Survey, Ministry for Conservation, 1983.

Hakluyt, R., *Voyages in Search of the North-West Passage*. London: Cassell & Company, 1886.

Hart, L.A., 'Positive Effects of Animals for Psychosocially Vulnerable People: a Turning Point for Delivery', in A. Fine (ed.), *Animal-assisted Therapy: Theoretical Foundations and Practical Guidelines* (3rd ed.), Boston: Elsevier Science and Technology, 2010, pp. 59–84.

Headey, B., and Grabka, M.M., 'Pets and Human Health in Germany and Australia: National Longitudinal Results', *Social Indicators Research*, vol. 80, no. 2, 2007, pp. 297-311. doi.org/10.1007/s11205-005-5072-z.

Heeres, J.E., *Het aandeel der Nederlanders in de ontdekking van Australie 1606-1765 — The Part Borne by the Dutch in the Discovery of Australia 1606-1765*. London: Royal Dutch Geographical Society, 1899.

Hill, Anthony, *Animal Heroes*. Camberwell, Victoria: Penguin, 2005.

Howard, A.J., 'Hall's Heelers', in R.M. Warner (ed.), *Over-Halling the Colony: George Hall, Pioneer*. Sydney: Australian Documents Library, 1990, pp. 121-126.

Hu, Yaowu, et al., 'Earliest Evidence for Commensal Processes of Cat Domestication', *Proceedings of the National Academy of Sciences*, vol. 111, no. 1, 2014, pp. 116–120.

Idriess, Ion, *Horrie the wog-dog: with the A.I.F. in Egypt, Greece, Crete and Palestine*. Sydney: Angus and Robertson, 1945.

Jackson, S.M., Groves, C.P., et al., 'The Wayward Dog: is the Australian Native Dog or Dingo a Distinct Species?' *Zootaxa*, vol. 4317, no. 2, 2017, pp. 201-224.

Jackson, S.M., Fleming, P.J.S., et al., 'Taxonomy of the Dingo: It's an ancient dog.' *Australian Zoologist*, vol. 41, no. 3, 2021, pp. 347–357. doi.org/10.7882/AZ.2020.049.

Jensen, David, *Huskies of the Heroic Era of Antarctic Exploration*. Norwich: The Erskine Press, 2018.

Johnson, Chris N., and Wallach, Arian D., 'The Virtuous Circle: Predator-Friendly Farming and Ecological Restoration in Australia', *Restoration Ecology*, vol. 24, no. 6, 2016, pp. 821–826.

Johnson, Helen, 'The Portrayal of the Dog on Greek Vases', *The Classical Weekly*, vol. 12, no. 27, 1919, pp. 209-213.

Jones, Rhys, 'Tasmanian Aborigines and Dogs', *Mankind*, vol. 7, no. 4, 1970, pp. 256-271.

Kaleski, Robert, 'Cattle Dogs', *Agricultural Gazette of New South Wales*, vol. 14, August, 1903, pp. 752-758.

— *Australian Barkers and Biters* (2nd ed.). Sydney: The Endeavour Press, 1933.

Karen, M.A., Blascovich, J., et al., 'Presence of Human Friends and Pet Dogs as Moderators of Autonomic Responses to Stress in Women', *Journal of Personality and Social Psychology*, vol. 61, no. 4, 1991, pp. 582-589.

Kitchell, Kenneth F. Jr, 'Man's Best Friend? The Changing Role of the Dog in Greek Society' [conference presentation], *Man and Animals in Antiquity: Proceedings of the Conference at the Swedish Institute in Rome*, Rome, 2004.

Kolig, E., 'Notes and Comments: Aboriginal Man's Best Foe?' *Mankind*, vol. 9, no. 2, 1973, pp. 122-123.

Koungoulos L., and Fillios, M. 'Hunting dogs down under? On the Aboriginal use of tame dingoes in dietary game acquisition and its relevance to Australian prehistory', *Journal of Anthropological Archaeology*, vol. 58, 2020. doi:10.1016/j.jaa.2020.101146.

Krol, William, 'Training the Combat and Operational Stress Control Dog: an Innovative Modality for Behavioral Health', U.S. *Army Medical Department Journal*, April-June, 2012, pp. 46-50.

Larson, G., Karlsson, E.K., et al., 'Rethinking Dog Domestication by Integrating Genetics, Archeology, and Biogeography', *Proceedings of the National Academy of Sciences*, vol. 109, no. 23, 2012, pp. 8878-8883.

Ledingham, Rod, *The ANARE Antarctic Dog Driver's Manual*, Australia: Xlibris, 2016.

Letnic, M., et al., 'Does a Top-Predator Provide an Endangered Rodent with Refuge from an Invasive Mesopredator?', *Animal Conservation*, vol. 12, no. 4, 2009, pp. 302–312.

Letnic, M., Fillios, M., et al., 'The Arrival and Impact of the Dingo', in A. Glen and C. Dickman (eds.), *Carnivores of Australia: Past, Present and Future*. Collingwood, Victoria: CSIRO Publishing, 2014, pp. 55-69.

Lurgi, M., et al., 'Eradicating Abundant Invasive Prey Could Cause Unexpected and Varied Biodiversity Outcomes: The Importance of Multispecies Interactions', *Journal of Applied Ecology*, vol. 55, no. 5, 2018, pp. 2396–2407.

Macintosh, N.G.W., 'A 3,000 Years Old Dingo From Shelter 6 (Fromm's Landing, South Australia)', *Proceedings of the Royal Society of Victoria*, vol. 77, 1964, pp. 498-507.

Macquarie Dictionary. 7th edition. Sydney, New South Wales, Australia: Macquarie Dictionary Publishers, 2017.

Mathews, Gregory, *The Birds of Australia*, London: Witherby, 1910–1927.

Melbourne Zoological Gardens, minutes of a meeting of the full board, 25 August 1950.

Mills, C.H., Wijas, B., et al., 'Two alternate states: shrub, bird and mammal assemblages differ on either side of the Dingo Barrier Fence', *Australian Zoologist*, vol. 41, no. 3, 2021, pp. 534–549. doi.org/10.7882/AZ.2021.005.

Moonie, Patrick, 'Memories of Dog Sledging at Mawson', *Aurora*, vol. 8, no. 1, 1988, pp. 38–45.

Mubanga, M., et al., 'Dog Ownership and the Risk of Cardiovascular Disease and Death – a Nationwide Cohort Study', *Scientific Reports*, vol. 7, 2017.

Mulvaney, K., 'What to do on a Rainy Day: Reminiscences of Mirruwung and Gadjerong Artists', *Rock Art Research*, vol. 13, no. 1, 1996, pp. 3-20.

National Archives of Australia: Antarctic Division; P1556, Files containing Antarctic Station Reports with Station Log Books interspersed, chronological series, 1947-; Report on Dogs – Mawson 1954; Report on Dogs [Huskies] - Mawson 1954 - ANARE [Australian National Antarctic Research Expedition]; 1954-1962; Davis 1962 (12); Davis ANARE (Australian National Antarctic Research Expedition) Station - Dogs and Sledging Report - by N. Trott – 1962.

National Library of Australia, 'What We Collect,' *National Library of Australia*, nla.gov.au/about-us/corporate-documents/policy-and-planning/collection-development-policy/what-we-collect.

Newsome, A.E., Corbett, L.K., et al., 'The Identity of the Dingo I. Morphological Discriminants of Dingo and Dog Skulls', *Australian Journal of Zoology*, vol. 28, no. 4, 1980, pp. 615-625.

Newsome, A.E., Catling, P.C., et al., 'Two Ecological Universes Separated by the Dingo Barrier Fence in Semi-Arid Australia: Interactions Between Landscapes, Herbivory and Carnivory, With and Without Dingoes', *Rangeland Journal*, vol. 23, no. 1, 2001, pp. 71-98.

Newsome, T. M., Ballard, G.A., et al., 'Resolving the value of the dingo in ecological restoration', *Restoration Ecology*, vol. 23, no. 3, 2015, pp. 201-208. doi.org/10.1111/REC.12186.

Newton, Gael, *Shades of Light. Photography and Australia 1839-1988*. Canberra: Australian National Gallery, 1988.

Olsen, S. and Olsen, J. 'The Chinese Wolf,

Ancestor of New World Dogs,' *Science*, vol. 197, no. 4303, 1977, pp. 533-535.

Oskarsson, M.C., Klütsch, C.F., et al., 'Mitochondrial DNA data indicate an introduction through Mainland Southeast Asia for Australian dingoes and Polynesian domestic dogs', *Proceedings. Biological sciences*, vol. 279, no. 1730, 2012, pp. 967–974. doi.org/10.1098/rspb.2011.1395.

Pardoe, C., 'Dogs changed the world,' *National Dingo News*, spring 1996, pp. 19-29.

Pardoe, C., and Tacon, P., 'Dogs Make Us Human', *Nature Australia*, vol. 27, no. 4, 2002, pp. 52-61.

Parsons, Tony, *The Kelpie. The definitive guide to the Australian working dog*. Camberwell, Vic.: Viking, 2010.

Peat, Neville, *Snow Dogs*. Christchurch, NZ: Whitcoulls Publishers, 1978.

Pedlar, Don, 'Dogs and Other Mascots', *Sabretache*, vol. 36, no. 1, 1995, pp. 30–33.

Perry, Roland, *Horrie the war dog*. Sydney: Allen & Unwin, 2013.

Phelan, S., *Conducting Dog Health Programs in Indigenous Communities: A Veterinary Guide*. Larrakia Country, Northern Territory: Animal Management in Rural and Remote Indigenous Communities (AMRRIC), 2007.

Phillip, J., ' The Waterfinders. A cultural history of the Australian dingo', *Australian Zoologist*, vol. 41, no. 3, 2021, pp. 593-607.

—, 'The Dingo Barrier Fence: Presenting the case to decommission the world's longest environmental barrier in the United Nations Decade on Ecosystem Restoration 2021–2030', *Biologia Futura*, vol. 73, no. 1, 2022, pp. 9-27. doi: 10.1007/s42977-021-00106-z

Polheber, John, and Matchock, Robert, 'The Presence of a Dog Attenuates Cortisol and Heart Rate in the Trier Social Stress Test Compared to Human Friends', *Journal of Behavioral Medicine*, vol. 37, no. 5, 2014, pp. 860–867

Pople, A.R., et al., 'Trends in the Numbers of Red Kangaroos and Emus on Either Side of the South Australian Dingo Fence: Evidence for Predator Regulation?' *Wildlife Research*, vol. 27, no. 3, 2000, pp. 269–276.

Prowse, Thomas A.A., et al., 'Ecological and Economic Benefits to Cattle Rangelands of Restoring an Apex Predator', *Journal of Applied Ecology*, vol. 52, no. 2, 2014, pp. 455–466.

Purcell, Brad, *Dingo*. Clayton South, Victoria: CSIRO Publishing, 2010.

Pyper, W., 'Antarctic Place Names Go to the Dogs', *Australian Antarctic Magazine*, no. 33, December 2017, p. 24.

Quartermaine, Peter and National Library of Australia, *Gundagai Album: early photographs of an Australian country town*. Canberra: NLA, 1976.

Rawson, Samuel *[Diaries and Papers], [1831-1857]*, National Library of Australia, MS 204.

Registrar-General's Office, *Statistics of the Colony of Victoria for the Year 1864*. Melbourne: John Ferres, Government Printer, 1866.

Ritvo, Harriet, *The Animal Estate*. Cambridge, Massachusetts: Harvard University Press, 1989.

— 'Pride and Pedigree: The Evolution of the Victorian Dog Fancy', *Victorian Studies*, vol.29, no.2, 1986, pp.227–253.

Robinson, Shelagh, *Huskies in Harness*. Kenthurst, NSW: Kangaroo Press, 1995.

Rose, Deborah Bird, *Dingo Makes Us Human: Life and Land in an Aboriginal Australian Culture*. Cambridge: Cambridge University Press, 1992.

Ryan, J.S., 'Plotting an Isogloss—the Location and Types of Aboriginal Names for Native Dog in New South Wales', *Oceania*, vol. 35, no. 2, 1964, pp.111–123.

Savolainen, P., Zhang, Y., et al., 'Genetic Evidence for an East Asian Origin of Domestic Dogs,' *Science*, vol. 298, 2002, pp. 1610-1613.

Savolainen P., Leitner T., et al., 2004. 'A detailed picture of the origin of the Australian dingo, obtained from the study of mitochondrial DNA', *Proceedings of the National Academy of Sciences of the USA*, vol 101, no. 33, 2004, pp. 12387–12390. doi:10.1073/pnas.0401814101.

Schroeder, F.E.H., 'Say Cheese! The Revolution in the Aesthetics of Smiles', *Journal of Popular Culture*, vol. 32, no. 2, 1998.

Scott, Eva, *Rupert Prince Palatine*, Westminster, UK: A. Constable & Co., 1899.

Scott, J.P., and Fuller, J.L., *Genetics and the Social Behavior of the Dog*. Chicago: University of Chicago Press, 1965.

Senior, K., Chenhall, R., et al., 'Dogs and people in Aboriginal communities: Exploring the relationship within the context of the social determinants of health', *Environmental Health: The Journal of the Australian Institute of Environmental Health*, vol. 6, 2006, pp. 39-46.

Shaw, George, *Musei Leveriani explicatio, anglica et latina/ Museum Leverianum, containing select specimens from the museum of the late Sir Ashton Lever, Kt, with descriptions in Latin and English*, vol. II, London: Impensis Jacobi Parkinson, 1792.

Shipman, P., *The Animal Connection: A New Perspective on What Makes Us Human*. New York: W.W. Norton & Company, 2011.

Skoglund, P., Ersmark, E., et al., 'Ancient Wolf Genome Reveals an Early Divergence of Domestic Dog Ancestors and Admixture into High-Latitude Breeds,' *Current Biology*, vol. 25, no. 11, 2015, pp. 1515-1519.

Smith, Bradley (ed.), *The Dingo Debate*. Clayton South, Victoria: CSIRO Publishing, 2015.

Smith, B.P., Appleby, R.G., et al., 'Co-existing with dingoes: Challenges and solutions to implementing non-lethal management', *Australian Zoologist*, June 2021 vol. 41, no. 3, 2021, pp. 491–510. doi.org/10.7882/AZ.2020.024.

Smith, B.P., Cairns, K.M., et al., 'Taxonomic Status of the Australian Dingo: the Case for Canis dingo, Meyer, 1793', *Zootaxa*, vol. 4564, no. 1, 2019, pp. 173-197.

Spira, H.R. (ed.), *An Historical Record of Australian Kennel Controls*. Melbourne: Australian National Kennel Council, 1988.

Statistics of the Colony of Victoria for the Year 1864. Melbourne: John Ferres, Government Printer, 1866.

Takashima, Gregg K., and Day, Michael J., 'Setting the One Health Agenda and the Human-Companion Animal Bond', *International Journal of Environmental Research and Public Health*, vol. 11, no. 11, 2014, pp. 11110–20.

Tacon, P., and Pardoe, C., 'Dogs make us human', *Natura Australia*, vol. 27, no. 4, 2002, pp. 52-62.

Terry, Michael, *Across Unknown Australia*. London: Herbert Jenkins Ltd, 1925.

— *Through a Land of Promise: With Gun, Car and Camera in the Heart of Northern Australia*. London: Herbert Jenkins Ltd, 1927.

— *Hidden Wealth and Hiding People*. London: Putnam, 1931.

— *Sun and Sand*. London: Michael Joseph Ltd., 1937.

— *The Last Explorer: The Autobiography of Michael Terry*, FRGS, FRGSA, compiled by C. Barnard. Rushcutters Bay, NSW: Australian National University Press, 1987.

Thomas, Keith, *Man and the Natural World. Changing Attitudes in England 1500-1800*. Harmondsworth: Penguin Books, 1983.

Thomson, Peter, 'The Behavioural Ecology of Dingoes in North-Western Australia. III Hunting and Feeding Behaviour, and Diet', *Wildlife Research*, vol. 19, no. 5, 1992, pp. 531–541.

Tranah, Gregory J., et al., 'Domestic and Farm-Animal Exposures and Risk of Non-Hodgkin's Lymphoma in a Population-Based Study in the San Francisco Bay Area', *Cancer Epidemiology*, Biomarkers & Prevention, vol. 17, no. 9, 2008, pp. 2382–2387.

Victoria: Crown land licenses, vol. II. Melbourne, John Ferres, Government Printer, 1856.

Vigne, J.D., et al., 'Early Taming of the Cat in Cyprus', *Science*, vol. 304, no. 5668, 2004, p. 259.

Vilà, C., Savolainen, P., et al., 'Multiple and Ancient Origins of the Domestic Dog', *Science*, vol. 276, no. 5319, 1997, pp. 1687-1689.

vonHoldt, Bridgett M., et al., 'Structural Variants in Genes Associated with Human Williams-Beuren Syndrome Underlie Stereotypical Hypersociability in Domestic Dogs', *Science Advances*, vol. 3, no. 7, 2017

von Stephanitz, M. [translated by J. Schwabacher], *The German Shepherd Dog in Word and Picture*, Jena, Germany: Anton Kampfe, 1923.

Wallace, R., *The Australians at the Boer War*,

Canberra: Australian War Memorial, 1976.

Wallach Arian D., et al., 'More than Mere Numbers: The Impact of Lethal Control on the Social Stability of a Top-Order Predator', *PLoS One*, vol. 4, no. 9, 2009, pp. 1–8.

Walsh, F., 'Human-Animal Bonds I: The Relational Significance of Companion Animals', *Family Process*, vol. 48, no. 4, 2009, pp.462–480.

Walton, Kevin, and Atkinson, Rick, *Of Dogs and Men. Fifty Years in the Antarctic*. Malvern Wells, UK: Images Publishing, 1996.

Wang, G., Zhai, W., et al., 'The Genomics of Selection in Dogs and the Parallel Evolution Between Dogs and Humans,' *Nature Communications*, vol. 4, 2013. doi.org/10.1038/ncomms2814, 2013.

Warburton, Eliot G., *Memoirs of Prince Rupert and the Cavaliers including their private correspondence*. London: Richard Bentley, 1849.

Wells, D.L., 'The Effects of Animals on Human Health and Well-Being', *Journal of Social Issues*, vol. 65, no. 3, 2009, pp. 523–543.

Willoughby, Anne-Louise, *Nora Heysen: a portrait*. Fremantle, WA: Fremantle Press, 2019.

Wisdom Health, *Murray River Retriever Genetic Study* (report), Second edition 2018.

Newspapers

The Advertiser (Adelaide)
The Advocate (Burnie, Tasmania)
The Australasian (Melbourne)
The Agricultural Gazette of New South Wales
The Argus (Melbourne)
Australian Town and Country Journal (Sydney)
The Bendigo Independent
The Brisbane Courier
The Bunbury Herald and Blackwood Express
The Bunyip (Gawler, South Australia)
The Burrangong Argus (New South Wales)
The Carcoar Chronicle (New South Wales)
The Courier-Mail (Brisbane)
Daily Advertiser (Wagga Wagga)
The Daily News (Perth)
Daily Telegraph (Launceston)
Daily Telegraph (Sydney)
The Herald (Melbourne)
The Horsham Times
Kalgoorlie Western Argus
The Land (Sydney)
Leader (Melbourne)
Lithgow Mercury
The Mail (Adelaide)
The Mercury (Hobart)
The Mirror (Sydney)
The Mirror of Australia (Sydney)
Mudgee Guardian and North-Western Representative
News (Adelaide)
The News Tribune (Tacoma, United States)
The Northern Argus (Clare, South Australia)
Nowra Leader
The Pioneer (South Australia)
The Queenslander (Brisbane)
The Register (Adelaide)
The Sydney Mail and New South Wales Advertiser
Sydney Mail
The Sydney Morning Herald
The Sydney Stock and Station Journal
The Sun (Sydney)
The Sunday Times (Perth)
Townsville Daily Bulletin
Truth (Brisbane)
Warialda Standard and Northern Districts' Advertiser (New South Wales)
Warrnambool Standard
Western Mail (Perth)

List of illustrations

Introduction

Chapter 1: By Our Sides

Chapter 2: The Dingo

Lawlor, *Fraser Island Dingo Yawning Showing Amazing Teeth*, Shutterstock image 1729800982.

Chapter 3: On the Farm

pp72—73 Bill Brindle, Australian News and Information Bureau, *Kelpie Working Sheep in a Yard*, 1955, nla.cat-vn4588605; **p74** Michael Terry, *Charlie Standing next to His Utility Truck and Dog, Alice Springs, Northern Territory*, 1961, nla.cat-vn6980467; **p77** Arthur Esam, *Rounding up Sheep for Shearing*, 1895, nla.cat-vn687154; **p78** John Crowther, Australian News and Information Bureau, *Border Collies in the Back of a Ute at National Sheep Dog Trials, Canberra*, 1964, nla.cat-vn4589036; **p81** *Jack Gallagher, Australian Bred Border Collie Sheep Dog with Farmer, Winners of Cooper Trophy Utility Trial*, 1949, nla.cat-vn4589514; **p82** *Bruce Postle, Binnie the Kelpie Standing on the Back of a Motorbike Ridden by his Owner, Jon Duffy, at Balargorang Park, Taminick, Victoria*, 1992, nla.cat-vn4579121; **pp86—87** *Sheepdogs Herding Sheep in the Saleyard at Homebush, New South Wales*, 1925, nla.cat-vn6192076, courtesy Fairfax Syndication; **p89** Charles Gabriel, *Man, Woman and Dog in a Garden, Gundagai, New South Wales*, between 1887 and 1927, nla.cat-vn730917; **p90** Keith Byron, Australian News and Information Bureau, *Tim Austin on His Motorcycle with Elfin vale Kelpie Studs Riding as Passengers, on His Farm in the Western District of Victoria*, 1967, nla.cat-vn4589010; **p95** Bruce Postle, *Farm Dog Bo Taking a Flying Leap up to a Hay Bale on the Back of a Truck, Moorabool, Victoria*, 1991, nla.cat-vn4579127; **pp98—99** Bill Brindle, Australian News and Information Bureau, *An Australian Cattle Dog Bails up a Group of Jersey Cows*, 1960s, nla.cat-vn4588771; **p100** Bill Brindle, Australian News and Information Bureau, *Top Breeder Trainer, Lionel Braithwaite, Introducing a Cattle Dog Puppy to a Stud Jersey Cow*, 1964, nla.cat-vn4588699; **p103** Darren Clark, *Robert Atkins and His Dog Moofty Walking Lambs Ready for Market*, 2015, Libraries Tasmania, NS5636/1/1; **p104** *William Smith with Dog Nell, Mrs Mick Sullivan, John Maguire, Mrs William Sullivan at Sullwood*, c.1906, nla.cat-vn1080055; **p109** Alf Scott Broad, *Australian Sports – Hunting the Emu*, 1886, nla.cat-vn2660574.

Chapter 4: Other Australians

pp110—111 Australian News and Information Bureau, *Cindy, Australian Silky Terrier and Kitten on a Table*, 1963, nla.cat-vn4590842; **p112** "Mickie" *Australian Terrier Sitting on a Wooden Chair in Garden*, c.1910, State Library of Victoria, H83.94/160; **p117** David Nemirovksy, *Tenterfield Terrier 01*, 2011, Wikimedia Commons; **p118** *Man and Dog at Gate to the Railed Veranda of Cottage, Hill End, New South Wales*, c.1872, nla.cat-vn4740613; **p121** *Clarence Bernhardt, Dog Sitting on a Railing, South Australia*, 1936, nla.cat-vn4087565.

Chapter 5: Australia's Antarctic Huskies

pp122—123 Frank Hurley, *Tom Crean Rears an Antarctic Family – Sally's Quadruplets*, c.1915, nla.cat-vn92337; **p124** J.W. Beattie, *Expeditionary Member and Sled Dogs on Board the Southern Cross Prior to Leaving for Antarctica, Hobart*, 1898, nla.cat-vn6007166; **p127** Frank Hurley, *Shakespeare, the Leader of My Team and the Most Sagacious Animal of the Pack*, c.1915, nla.cat-vn90543; **p128** Percy Spiden, *Sailor from the Commandant Charcot with a Husky*, c.1951, State Library of Victoria, H2008.121/31; **pp132—133** *Huskies Resting on Sledging Trip, Antarctica*, 1950s, State Library of New South Wales, PXE 731/1876-1915; **p135** Charles J. Page, *Australian Antarctic Territory, Weighing a Husky on the Last Husky Run*, 1993, nla.cat-vn3798263; **p136** *An Explorer with George the Husky*, c.1955, nla.cat-vn6001665; **pp140—141** Charles J. Page, *Australian Antarctic Territory, Last Husky Run with ANARE Club Flag*, 1993, nla.cat-vn3798262; **p142** *Andrew Watson with a Dog, Antarctica*, between 1911 and 1914, nla.cat-vn4925933; **p145** Frank Hurley, *Ocean Camp, Weddell Sea, with Two Dogs Looking at Camera and Penguins*, c.1915, nla.cat-489319.

Chapter 6: Mascots

pp146—147 *Mascot*, c.1940, State Library of Victoria, H99.201/1464, **p148** *"Bushie" The Celebrated Australian War Dog*, c.1899, courtesy Katherine Kovacic; **p151** *Horrie, the Four-legged Mascot and Campaigner Attached to the 2/1st Machine Gun Battalion*, 1941, Australian War Memorial, 076877; **p152** *"Bushie", a Collie Dog, with Members of the 3rd Victorian Bushmen Contingent*, 1900, Australian War Memorial, P11043.001; **p154** *Nelson, S.A. Regimental Pet, Transvaal War*, c.1900, State Library of South Australia, BRG 216/12/11; **p157** *Great Dane Pup, Mascot of 2/13th Battalion, Joins Parade at Katoomba*, c.1943, State Library of

Victoria, H99.201/5311; **pp158—159** *Victoria Barracks Girls with the Only Dog to Enter the Barracks, Brisbane*, 1945, State Library of Queensland, negative number: 44052; **p162** Darge Photographic Company, *Studio Portrait of W. Carroll with a Dog*, 1916, Australian War Memorial, DA16065; **p164** Rose Stereographs, *Soldiers from the Australian Expeditionary Force with Their Mascot, Broadmeadows, Victoria*, 1914, nla.cat-vn6573448; **p167** Australian News and Information Bureau, *Children Form an Impromptu Guard of Honour for a Visitor to Canberra*, 1958, nla.cat-vn6186410.

Chapter 7: Outback Dogs

pp168—169 Michael Terry, *Two Expedition Members and the Expedition's Dog, Spot, at a Camp Table in the Warburton Ranges, Western Australia*, 1931, nla.cat-vn6577181; **p170** *'Tis a Hot Day on Patrol and Water is Scarce*, c.1935, nla.cat-vn3298444; **p173** S.A. White, *A Member of Captain S.A. White's Party and His Dog Seated on a Camel during the Trip to the Everard and Musgrave Ranges, Central Australia*, 1913, nla.cat-vn4652647; **p174** *Francis Birtles and His Dog Camped beside the Car Having a Drink, Arnhem Land*, between 1899 and 1928, nla.cat-vn3301921; **p177** *Clive Birtles at the Wheel of the Car with the Dog, Wowser*, c.1918, nla.cat-vn3303076; **p178** *Wowser's Grave Site, Northern Queensland*, c.1920, nla.cat-vn6097546; **p181** Roy Fry, *Francis Birtles and Dinkum the Cattle Dog Riding a Camel, Heavitree Gap, Alice Springs, Northern Territory*, 1921, nla.cat-vn6419799; **p182** *Francis Birtles' Dog Dinkum behind the Wheel of a Car*, c.1924, nla.cat-vn5399781; **p185** *Francis Birtles' Dog Yowie on a Rock Overlooking Alice Springs Railway, Northern Territory*, c.1920, nla.cat-vn5399830; **p??** *Adventurer Francis Birtles in His Vehicle Surrounded by a Crowd on His Return to Sydney from England*, 1928, nla.cat-vn6267123, courtesy Fairfax Syndication; **p186** Michael Terry, *Morris Commercial Truck Descending a Gully with the Expedition's Dog, Eccetry, Sitting on the Back, Mount Dockrell, Western Australia*, 1928, nla.cat-vn6576619; **p191 (top)** Michael Terry, *The Expedition Team's Dog Eccerty Digging Holes in Sandy Soil, Western Australia*, 1928, nla.cat-vn6249032; **p191 (bottom)** Michael Terry, *Eccetry, the Expedition's Dog, in Front of a Morris Commercial Truck at Margaret River, Western Australia*, 1928, nla.cat-vn6576622; **pp192—193** Michael Terry, *Expedition Member Bill Bird inside a Tent with Spot the Dog, Western Australia*, 1931, nla.cat-vn6577187; **p196** Michael Terry, *Expedition Member Bill Bird Sitting in a Morris Commercial Truck with a Dog, Central Australia*, c.1930, nla.cat-vn6577026.

Conclusion

p199 *Rosemary James with a Dog, Cobbity, New South Wales*, 1936, nla.cat-vn6219930, courtesy Fairfax Syndication; **p200** Keith Byron, Australian News and Information Bureau, *A Drover and His Three Cattle Dogs Jog along behind a Herd of Cattle during an Annual Migration Drive near the Victorian Section of the Australian Alps*, 1966, nla.cat-vn4589905; **p202—203** Francis Reiss, *Paddy Japaljarri Stewart from the Warlukurlangu Artists Aboriginal Association at the Yuendumu Art Centre, Yuendumu*, 2003, nla.cat-vn3308281, courtesy June Orford.

Acknowledgements

It's always a delight to talk about dogs. Thank you to everyone who has enthusiastically discussed breeds, training, genetics and just about every aspect of dogs in Australia with me. In particular I would like to extend my heartfelt thanks to:

Karen Rawady, Melbourne Zoo

Lyn Watson, Dingo Discovery Sanctuary and Research Centre

Michelle Griffiths, Wiradjuri descendant

Karen Bell, Murray River Retriever historian (sadly deceased)

The Murray River Retriever Association Inc.

The Koolie Club of Australia

Thank you also to the whole National Library of Australia publishing team for following me deep into the Library's collections and embracing this project with such gusto.